Systematic Approach to Basic English Composition

Akihiko Haisa
Gary Bourke
Joanne Sato

Asahi Press

音声再生アプリ「リスニング・トレーナー」を使った音声ダウンロード

朝日出版社開発のアプリ、「リスニング・トレーナー（リストレ）」を使えば、教科書の音声をスマホ、タブレットに簡単にダウンロードできます。どうぞご活用ください。

◉ アプリ【リスニング・トレーナー】の使い方

《アプリのダウンロード》

App Store または Google Play から「リスニング・トレーナー」のアプリ（無料）をダウンロード

App Storeは
こちら▶

Google Playは
こちら▶

《アプリの使い方》

① アプリを開き「コンテンツを追加」をタップ
② 画面上部に【15707】を入力しDoneをタップ

音声ストリーミング配信 》》》

この教科書の音声は、右記ウェブサイトにて無料で配信しています。

https://text.asahipress.com/free/english/

はじめに

　本書は、英語を話したり書いたりするのに必要な英作文能力を基礎からしっかり身につけることを目標としたテキストです。英語を聞いたり読んだりする作業では、単語から推測しながら何となく意味をつかむこともできますが、話す・書くといったアウトプットの作業では、文法がしっかりできていないとなかなか文を組み立てることができません。そのため、英作文に苦手意識を持っている学生さんも多いようです。

　本書の特徴は、主語と動詞を意識しながら英作文を試みることです。英語は語順が決まっている言語であり、副詞や副詞的な語句や文のまとまりで始まる英文を除いて、ほぼ常に「主語＋動詞」で文が始まります。そして、主語に続く動詞の部分が、否定文、疑問文、時制、助動詞との結合、などにより様々な形となって動詞のまとまりを作ります。まず主語を述べ、伝えたい内容に沿って動詞のまとまりをつなげることができれば最初の一歩はクリアです。その後に補語や目的語を続けることで英文を完成させることができます。本書では、全ての基本例文で、動詞のまとまりに下線を引くことで、その意識化を図りました。

　本書のもう1つの特徴は、各ユニットで扱う文や文章にトピックを設けたことです。トピックは、企業の社内研修などで会話術としてよく引用される「きどにたちかけせし衣食住」という12個の頭文字が示す話題を、ユニット毎に扱ってみました。具体的には「き（気候）・ど（道楽）・に（ニュース）・た（旅）・ち（知人）・か（家庭）・け（健康）・せ（性）・し（仕事）・衣・食・住」というもので、日常会話で頻繁に使われる話題を網羅しています。本書で学習することで、文法だけでなく、そうした日常の何気ない世間話や雑談で使える語彙や表現も一緒に身につけることができるよう工夫しました。

　Unit 1～6 では、英語力の最も基本である動詞の変形に焦点を当てながら、それぞれの文法項目に沿って練習を積みます。また、Unit 8～13 では、主に不定詞、動名詞、分詞、接続詞、関係詞など、1つの文で動詞がもう1つ出てくるような英文に取り組みます。少しハードルは上がりますが、Unit 1～6 で学習した文法の基本をベースにしつつ、それを新たな英文構造に組み込むことで、やや複雑な文がしっかりアウトプットできるようになることを目指します。

　各ユニットは6ページで構成され、最初の2ページが基本例文の紹介、3ページ目が英文構造を把握する問題（英文構造把握問題）、4ページ目が基礎的な語句の並べ替え問題（基礎問題）、5ページ目がやや難度を高めた語句の並べ替え問題（発展問題）、そして6ページ目は、その課で扱うトピックを題材にした文章を読み、意味を考えながら文中の語句の並べ替えをする問題（文章理解問題）となっています。

　英文構造把握問題、基礎問題、発展問題では、参照すべき基本例文の番号がそれぞれの問題に付されているので、何がその問題のポイントなのかがわかるようになっています。また、前半の6ユニット、後半の6ユニットが終わったところで、それぞれ復習問題を設けました。復習問題では、学習した文法項目を再度扱いますが、異なったトピックとの組合せにしてみました。

　学生の皆さんが、本書での学習を通して、英文法の基礎を理解し、様々なトピックでのアウトプット能力を向上させることができたら幸いです。最後になりましたが、朝日出版社の朝日英一郎氏には企画の段階から貴重なご助言をいただき、大変お世話になりました。心からお礼申し上げます。

2022 年夏　著者

本書の特徴と使い方

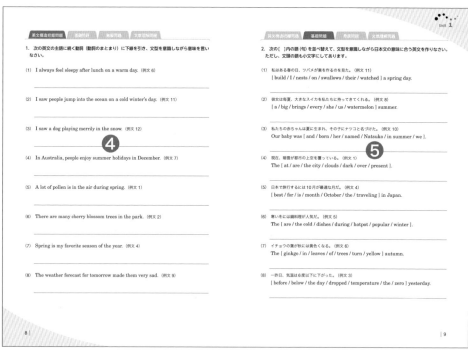

① 各課で扱う文法項目のポイントを簡潔に説明しています。その課がねらいとする
大きな枠組みを意識しながら基本例文を読んでみましょう。

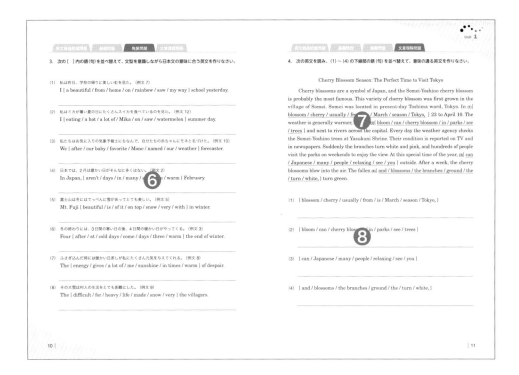

❷　その課で学ぶ文法項目に沿った基本例文を提示しています。基本例文はどれもユニット毎に設けられたテーマに関連する英文です。第三者に伝えたり問いかけたりするようなイメージで英文を読むと良いでしょう。全ての基本例文で動詞のまとまりに下線が引かれているので、主語と動詞のつながりを意識しながら英文構造を確認してみてください。

❸　基本例文にはネイティブスピーカーが読み上げた音声が用意されています。繰り返し聞いて基礎文法の復習をすると共に、苦手な発音の克服にも役立ててください。

❹　学習した文法項目を含む英文構造把握問題です。基本例文と同様に下線を引くことで、主語と目的語や補語をつなげる動詞のまとまりに着目してみましょう。それぞれの問題にはポイントとなる基本例文の番号が付されているので、参照しながら学習してみてください。

❺　基本例文で学習した内容をアウトプットにつなげるための並べ替え問題（基礎問題）です。まずは伝えたい日本文のメッセージから、主語は何か、それにつながる動詞のまとまりは何かを意識して英作文に取り組んでみてください。

❻　語彙や文法でやや難度を高めた並べ替え問題（発展問題）です。その課で学ぶ文法に加え、それ以前に学習した文法項目が含まれていたりするので復習にもなります。④⑤⑥の練習問題を解くことで学習内容の定着を図りましょう。

❼　そのユニットで扱っているトピックに関する短いパラグラフです。その課で学習した文法項目が多く含まれているので、復習を兼ねながらリーディング力を鍛えます。

❽　パラグラフを読みながら文中にある語句の並べ替えをする問題です。参照する日本文がないので、文章全体の意味を考えながら、その流れに沿って英作文をする力が鍛えられます。

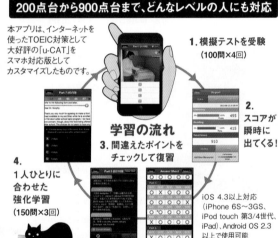

目 次

Systematic Approach to Basic English Composition

Akihiko Haisa
Gary Bourke
Joanne Sato

Asahi Press

unit 1

5文型（be動詞と一般動詞）

トピック ▶ 気候、季節

||| 解説 |||

　どの英文もSV、SVC、SVO、SVOO、SVOCの5つの文型に分類できますが、動詞にかかる副詞や副詞的な語句のまとまりがつくことでわかりにくくなってしまいます。ここでは副詞や副詞的な語句のまとまりを丸かっこでくくることで、S（主語）、V（動詞）、C（補語）、O（目的語）という文の主要素を明確にします。また動詞にはbe動詞と一般動詞があり、多くの場合、その前に主語が来て、その後に補語や目的語が続きます。動詞（動詞のまとまり）を意識しながら、それぞれの文型を学習しましょう。

🔊 2  **基本例文**

第1文型

S（主語）＋ V（be動詞）

1. He is (always) (in the garden) (on sunny days).
   ˢ ᵛ
   彼は（晴れた日には）（いつも）（庭に）いる。

   ＊この文型のbe動詞は「いる」「ある」という意味になります。

There ＋ V（be動詞）＋ S（主語）

2. There is a lot of snow (on the houses).
   ᵛ ˢ
   （家々には）たくさんの雪が 積もっている。

   ＊thereという副詞が文頭に来て、倒置になっていますが、定型表現として使えるようにしましょう。

S（主語）＋ V（一般動詞）

3. The sun rises (in the east).
   ˢ ᵛ
   太陽は（東から）昇る。

第2文型

S（主語）＋ V（be動詞）＋ C（名詞）　　S＝C

4. Her sister is a famous weather forecaster.
   ˢ ᵛ ᶜ
   彼女の姉/妹は 有名な気象予報士 です。

| S（主語）＋ V（be動詞）＋ C（形容詞） | S＝C |

5. It is very cold (today).

s　v　　　c

（今日は）とても 寒い です。

　*「be動詞＋形容詞」は本書では「動詞のまとまり」として扱っています。

| S（主語）＋ V（一般動詞）＋ C（形容詞） | S＝C |

6. Haruko (always) looks happy (on a sunny day).

s　　　　　v　　c

ハルコは（晴れた日には）（いつも）幸せそうに 見える。

　*「一般動詞＋形容詞」は本書では「動詞のまとまり」として扱っています。

第3文型

| S（主語）＋ V（一般動詞）＋ O（目的語） |

7. My brother likes spring (the best) (among the four seasons).

　s　　　v　　o

私の兄/弟は（四季の中では）春が（一番）好きだ。

第4文型

| S（主語）＋ V（一般動詞）＋ O（目的語）＋ O（目的語） |

8. Makoto gave Mikiko a lovely present (on Christmas Eve).

　s　　v　　o　　o

マコトは（クリスマスイブに）ミキコに すてきなプレゼントを あげた。

第5文型

| S（主語）＋ V（使役動詞 [make]）＋ O（名詞）＋ C（形容詞） | O＝C |

9. The warm spring sunshine makes me happy.

　　　　　s　　　　　v　　o　c

暖かい春の日差しが 私を 幸せに してくれる。

　*「使役動詞と形容詞」は本書では「動詞のまとまり」として扱っています。

| S（主語）＋ V（一般動詞 [callなど]）＋ O（名詞）＋ C（名詞） | O＝C |

10. My friends called the weather forecaster Ten-chan.

　s　　　v　　　o　　　　　　　c

私の友だちは その気象予報士を テンちゃんと 呼んだ。

| S（主語）＋ V（知覚動詞 [seeなど]）＋ O（名詞）＋ C（動詞の原形） | O＝C |

11. I saw a weather forecaster use a weather map on TV.

s　v　　　o　　　　　　c

私は 気象予報士が テレビで天気図を使うのを 見た。

| S（主語）＋ V（知覚動詞）＋ O（名詞）＋ C（動詞の現在分詞） | O＝C |

12. I heard him singing in the rain.

s　v　　o　　c

私は 彼が 雨の中で歌っているのを 聞いた。

1. 次の英文の主語に続く動詞（動詞のまとまり）に下線を引き、文型を意識しながら意味を言いなさい。

(1) I always feel sleepy after lunch on a warm day. （例文 6）

_____

(2) I saw people jump into the ocean on a cold winter's day. （例文 11）

_____

(3) I saw a dog playing merrily in the snow. （例文 12）

_____

(4) In Australia, people enjoy summer holidays in December. （例文 7）

_____

(5) A lot of pollen is in the air during spring. （例文 1）

_____

(6) There are many cherry blossom trees in the park. （例文 2）

_____

(7) Spring is my favorite season of the year. （例文 4）

_____

(8) The weather forecast for tomorrow made them very sad. （例文 9）

_____

英文構造把握問題　　**基礎問題**　　発展問題　　文章理解問題

2. 次の [　] 内の語 (句) を並べ替えて、文型を意識しながら日本文の意味に合う英文を作りなさい。
ただし、文頭の語も小文字にしてあります。

(1) 私はある春の日、ツバメが巣を作るのを見た。（例文 11）

[build / I / nests / on / swallows / their / watched] a spring day.

_____

(2) 彼女は毎夏、大きなスイカを私たちに持ってきてくれる。（例文 8）

[a / big / brings / every / she / us / watermelon] summer.

_____

(3) 私たちの赤ちゃんは夏に生まれ、その子にナツコと名づけた。（例文 10）

Our baby was [and / born / her / named / Natsuko / in summer / we].

_____

(4) 現在、暗雲が都市の上空を覆っている。（例文 1）

The [at / are / the city / clouds / dark / over / present].

_____

(5) 日本で旅行するには 10 月が最適な月だ。（例文 4）

[best / for / is / month / October / the / traveling] in Japan.

_____

(6) 寒い冬には鍋料理が人気だ。（例文 5）

The [are / the cold / dishes / during / hotpot / popular / winter].

_____

(7) イチョウの葉が秋には黄色くなる。（例文 6）

The [ginkgo / in / leaves / of / trees / turn / yellow] autumn.

_____

(8) 一昨日、気温は 6 度以下に下がった。（例文 3）

[before / below / the day / dropped / temperature / the / zero] yesterday.

_____

3. 次の [ ] 内の語(句)を並べ替えて、文型を意識しながら日本文の意味に合う英文を作りなさい。

(1) 私は昨日、学校の帰りに美しい虹を見た。（例文 7）

I [a beautiful / from / home / on / rainbow / saw / my way] school yesterday.

_____

(2) 私はミカが暑い夏の日にたくさんスイカを食べているのを見た。（例文 12）

I [eating / a hot / a lot of / Mika / on / saw / watermelon] summer day.

_____

(3) 私たちはお気に入りの気象予報士にちなんで、自分たちの赤ちゃんにモネと名づけた。（例文 10）

We [after / our baby / favorite / Mone / named / our / weather] forecaster.

_____

(4) 日本では、2 月は暖かい日がそんなに多くはない。（例文 2）

In Japan, [aren't / days / in / many / so / there / warm] February.

_____

(5) 富士山は冬にはてっぺんに雪があってとても美しい。（例文 5）

Mt. Fuji [beautiful / is / of it / on top / snow / very / with] in winter.

_____

(6) 冬の終わりには、3 日間の寒い日の後、4 日間の暖かい日がやってくる。（例文 3）

Four [after / at / cold days / come / days / three / warm] the end of winter.

_____

(7) ふさぎ込んだ時には暖かい日差しが私にたくさん元気を与えてくれる。（例文 8）

The [energy / gives / a lot of / me / sunshine / in times / warm] of despair.

_____

(8) その大雪は村人の生活をとても困難にした。（例文 9）

The [difficult / for / heavy / life / made / snow / very] the villagers.

_____

英文構造把握問題　基礎問題　発展問題　文章理解問題

4.　次の英文を読み、(1) ～ (4) の下線部の語 (句) を並べ替えて、意味の通る英文を作りなさい。

Cherry Blossom Season: The Perfect Time to Visit Tokyo

　　　Cherry blossoms are a symbol of Japan, and the Somei-Yoshino cherry blossom is probably the most famous. This variety of cherry blossom was first grown in the village of Somei. Somei was located in present-day Toshima ward, Tokyo. In (1)[blossom / cherry / usually from / is / March / season / Tokyo,] 23 to April 10. The weather is generally warmer, and we (2)[bloom / can / cherry blossom / in / parks / see / trees] and next to rivers across the capital. Every day the weather agency checks the Somei-Yoshino trees at Yasukuni Shrine. Their condition is reported on TV and in newspapers. Suddenly the branches turn white and pink, and hundreds of people visit the parks on weekends to enjoy the view. At this special time of the year, (3)[can / Japanese / many / people / relaxing / see / you] outside. After a week, the cherry blossoms blow into the air. The fallen (4)[and / blossoms / the branches / ground / the / turn / white,] turn green.

(1)　[blossom / cherry / usually from / is / March / season / Tokyo,]

_____

(2)　[bloom / can / cherry blossom / in / parks / see / trees]

_____

(3)　[can / Japanese / many / people / relaxing / see / you]

_____

(4)　[and / blossoms / the branches / ground / the / turn / white,]

_____

時制（現在形、過去形、未来形）

トピック　趣味、娯楽

‖‖ 解説 ‖‖

　Unit 2では時制を意識した英作文演習に取り組みます。動詞にはbe動詞と一般動詞があり、現在・過去・未来のことについて表現する際に、それぞれの動詞において規則性があります。基本例文では、主語と時制によってそれぞれの動詞がどのように変化するかを、動詞（動詞のまとまり）に下線を引くことで意識化します。また本課では、平叙文（肯定文・否定文）と疑問文の作り方も練習します。

◀》3  基本例文

`be動詞・現在形`

| am | 主語が「I」のとき

1. I <u>am</u> a big fan of that rock band.
   私はあのロックバンドの大ファンだ。
   *否定文：am not　　*疑問文：amを文頭に移動

| are | 主語が「we, you, they, その他の3人称複数の名詞」のとき

2. They <u>are good</u> at fishing in the river.
   彼らは川釣りが得意だ。
   *否定文：aren't　　*疑問文：areを文頭に移動

| is | 主語が「he, she, it, その他の3人称単数の名詞」のとき

3. Tsubasa <u>is</u> my favorite soccer player.
   ツバサは私の大好きなサッカー選手だ。
   *否定文：isn't　　*疑問文：isを文頭に移動

`be動詞・過去形`

| was | 主語が「I, he, she, it, その他の3人称単数の名詞」のとき

4. I <u>was excited</u> about my favorite musician's concert.
   私は好きなミュージシャンのコンサートに興奮した。
   *否定文：wasn't　　*疑問文：wasを文頭に移動

| were | 主語が「we, you, they, その他の3人称複数の名詞」のとき |

5. We <u>were</u> fearless skateboarders in our hometown.
   私たちは故郷では恐れ知らずのスケートボーダー<u>だった</u>。
   *否定文：weren't   *疑問文：were を文頭に移動

一般動詞・現在形

| 肯定文 | 主語が「I, we, you, they, その他の3人称複数の名詞」のとき |

6. I often <u>play</u> badminton with my friends in the park.
   私は公園でよく友だちとバドミントンを<u>する</u>。
   *否定文：don't ＋一般動詞の原形

| 疑問文 | 主語が「I, we, you, they, その他の3人称複数の名詞」のとき |

7. <u>Do</u> you often <u>play</u> cards with your classmates?
   あなたはよくクラスメートとトランプを<u>しますか</u>？

| 肯定文 | 主語が「he, she, it, その他の3人称単数の名詞」のとき |

8. Hanako often <u>goes</u> to the amusement park on holidays.
   ハナコは休日によく遊園地に<u>行く</u>。
   *否定文：doesn't ＋一般動詞の原形

| 疑問文 | 主語が「he, she, it, その他の3人称単数の名詞」のとき |

9. <u>Does</u> he often <u>read</u> books in his favorite cafe?
   彼はお気に入りのカフェでよく本を<u>読みますか</u>？

一般動詞・過去形

| 肯定文 | 全ての主語 |

10. I <u>belonged</u> to a tea ceremony club in my high school days.
    私は高校時代、茶道部に<u>所属していた</u>。
    *否定文：didn't ＋ 一般動詞の原形

| 疑問文 | 全ての主語 |

11. <u>Did</u> you <u>watch</u> the suspense movie on TV last night?
    昨夜、テレビでサスペンス映画を<u>見ましたか</u>？

be動詞/一般動詞・未来形

| (am/are/is) ＋ going to ＋ (be動詞/一般動詞の原形) |

12. I <u>am going to visit</u> the famous art museum in Gunma.
    私は群馬県の有名な美術館を<u>訪れる予定だ</u>。

1.　次の英文の主語に続く動詞（動詞のまとまり）に下線を引き、時制を意識しながら意味を言いなさい。

(1)　I'm not the best snowboarder in my family.（例文 1）

_____

(2)　We are keen fans of that Korean idol group.（例文 2）

_____

(3)　Were you a good baseball player in your high school days?（例文 5）

_____

(4)　Do you often read exciting novels in bed after dinner?（例文 7）

_____

(5)　Did you enjoy horseback riding during your school trip?（例文 11）

_____

(6)　She has a special interest in scuba diving near tropical islands.（例文 8）

_____

(7)　Yuka watched the horror movie with her boyfriend last week.（例文 10）

_____

(8)　Surfing is an attractive sport for people of all ages.（例文 3）

_____

2.　次の [ ] 内の語 (句) を並べ替えて、時制を意識しながら日本文の意味に合う英文を作りなさい。ただし、文頭の語も小文字にしてあります。

(1)　私は古いアメリカ映画、特にラブストーリーに興味がある。(例文 1)

[am / American / I / in / interested / movies / old], especially love stories.

(2)　私はたいてい夕食後に好きなテレビドラマを見る。(例文 6)

I [after / dramas / favorite / my / TV / usually / watch] dinner.

(3)　彼は自由時間によくネットサーフィンを楽しみますか？ (例文 9)

[does / enjoy / he / in / internet / often / surfing] his free time?

(4)　彼は将来、有名なミュージシャンになろうとしている。(例文 12)

[a / be / famous musician / going / he / is / to] in the future.

(5)　彼女はそのロックバンドのリードボーカルでしたか？ (例文 4)

[in / lead / the rock band / she / singer / the / was]?

(6)　レイコはあなたの高校では有名なテニス選手ですか？ (例文 3)

[a / in / is / player / Reiko / tennis / well-known] your high school?

(7)　ケンゴはその重要なサッカーの試合でゴールを決めた。(例文 10)

[a goal / important / in / Kengo / scored / soccer / the] match.

(8)　彼らはずいぶん前にニューヨークでプロのダンサーだった。(例文 5)

[dancers / in / a long / New York / professional / they / were] time ago.

3.　次の [　] 内の語（句）を並べ替えて、時制を意識しながら日本文の意味に合う英文を作りなさい。ただし、文頭の語も小文字にしてあります。

(1)　私たちは今年の夏、秋田の有名な花火大会を見に行く予定です。（例文 12）

We [are / display / a famous firework / going / in / to / watch] Akita this summer.

_____

(2)　あなたは東京で人気の商店街をよく散策しますか？（例文 7）

[around / do / often / popular / shopping / walk / you] districts in Tokyo?

_____

(3)　あなたは昨日、タマキが一人でカラオケボックスに入るのを見ましたか？（例文 11）

[did / enter / karaoke box / see / Tamaki / the / you] alone yesterday?

_____

(4)　彼は 1970 年代に最も人気のあるシンガーソングライターだった。（例文 4）

[during / he / the most / popular / singer-song writer / the / was] 1970s.

_____

(5)　彼女は月に 1 回お気に入りのショッピングモールで買い物を楽しむ。（例文 8）

She [at / enjoys / favorite / her / once / shopping / shopping mall] a month.

_____

(6)　彼女はよくお昼休みに友だちにギターのレッスンをしていますか？（例文 9）

[does / during / her friends / a guitar lesson / give / often / she] lunch break?

_____

(7)　最近、多くの若いカップルはスマホでオンラインゲームを楽しむ。（例文 6）

Recently, [enjoy / many / on / online games / playing / their / young couples] smartphones.

_____

(8)　カウボーイ映画は若者の間ではそんなに人気はない。（例文 2）

[among / aren't / cowboy / movies / popular / so / young] people.

_____

4. 次の英文を読み、（1）〜（4）の下線部の語（句）を並べ替えて、意味の通る英文を作りなさい。
ただし、文頭の語も小文字にしてあります。

A New Year, A New Hobby

Do you have a hobby? Do you want a new hobby? (1)[at / in / interested / school / sports / were / you]? For many Japanese people, April is the beginning of a new year, and many Japanese people think about starting a new hobby. Many young people play sports or musical instruments. (2)[the baseball / belonged / high / I / in / team / to] school, and many of my friends played in the school band. (3)[am / anymore / baseball / I / in / interested / not], but I am eager to find a new hobby. Nowadays, many people search online to find new hobbies. On the internet, they may find various popular hobbies according to age group and gender. Nowadays, more men and women are searching for hobbies to do at home. For example, women are interested in practicing yoga and reading manga, while more men are watching movies and learning to cook. I'm going to check the website and try to find a new hobby for spring. How (4)[a / are / find / going / new hobby / to / you]?

(1)　[at / in / interested / school / sports / were / you]

_____

(2)　[the baseball / belonged / high / I / in / team / to]

_____

(3)　[am / anymore / baseball / I / in / interested / not]

_____

(4)　[a / are / find / going / new hobby / to / you]

_____

unit 3 時制
（現在／過去進行形、現在完了形など）

トピック ▶ ニュース、情報

‖‖ 解説 ‖‖

　Unit 3でも時制を扱いますが、主に進行形（現在／過去）と現在完了形を使った表現に取り組みます。現在完了形は、日本語では主に経験、継続、完了の意味を持つので、その使い方に慣れましょう。これらの表現にも規則性があり、基本例文では動詞のまとまりに下線が引かれているので、その形式を意識化してみてください。また本課でも、それぞれの表現で平叙文（肯定文・否定文）と疑問文の作り方を練習します。

---

 4 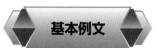 基本例文

現在進行形

肯定文 | 主語＋（am/are/is）＋動詞のing形

1. People on the train <u>are reading</u> the newspaper on their smartphones.
   電車に乗っている人々はスマホで新聞を<u>読んでいます</u>。
   ＊進行形は未来を意味するときもあります。

否定文 | 主語 ＋（am not/aren't/isn't）＋ 動詞のing形

2. Students <u>aren't using</u> their laptop computers in his English class.
   彼の英語の授業では生徒たちはノートパソコンを<u>使っていません</u>。

疑問文 | （Am/Are/Is）＋ 主語 ＋ 動詞のing形

3. <u>Are</u> you <u>watching</u> the news on TV now?
   あなたは今、テレビでニュースを<u>見ています</u>か？

過去進行形

肯定文 | 主語 ＋（was/were）＋ 動詞のing形

4. The trains in Tokyo <u>were running</u> on time as usual yesterday.
   昨日も東京の電車はいつも通り定刻に<u>走っていた</u>。

否定文	主語 ＋（wasn't／weren't）＋ 動詞のing形

5. I wasn't dozing during the lecture on that day.
　　私はその日、講義中に居眠りしていませんでした。

疑問文	（Was／Were）＋主語 ＋ 動詞のing形

6. Were you taking the online lesson at this time yesterday?
　　あなたは昨日のこの時間にオンライン授業を受けていましたか？

現在完了形

経験（肯定文）	主語 ＋（have／has）＋ 動詞の過去分詞

7. I have visited the TV station several times.
　　私は数回、そのテレビ局を訪問したことがある。

経験（否定文）	主語＋（haven't／hasn't）＋ 動詞の過去分詞

8. I haven't used this voice translation device before.
　　私は以前にこの音声翻訳機を使ったことがない。

　　*（have never／has never）とneverで否定文を作ることもあります。

経験（疑問文）	（Have／Has）＋ 主語 ＋ 動詞の過去分詞

9. Have you ever heard such a piece of exciting news?
　　あなたはかつてこんなにワクワクするニュースを聞いたことがありますか？

継続（肯定文）	主語 ＋（have／has）＋ 動詞の過去分詞

10. I have known the radio personality since childhood.
　　私は子供の頃からずっとそのラジオパーソナリティーを知っている。
　　*否定文、疑問文の作り方は、「経験」の例文と同様です。

完了（肯定文）	主語 ＋（have, has）＋ 動詞の過去分詞

11. I have just written the research paper for my seminar.
　　私はゼミの研究論文をちょうど書いたところだ。
　　*否定文、疑問文の作り方は、「経験」の例文と同様です。

現在完了進行形

肯定文	主語 ＋（have／has）＋ been ＋ 動詞のing形

12. I have been playing online games for six hours.
　　私は6時間オンラインゲームをずっとやり続けている。

1. 次の英文の主語に続く動詞（動詞のまとまり）に下線を引き、時制を意識しながら意味を言いなさい。

(1) I have never watched news programs in English on cable TV. （例文 8）

_____

(2) Have you ever played *shogi* with an AI robot somewhere before? （例文 9）

_____

(3) Have you written the first draft for the essay contest yet? （例文 11）

_____

(4) Mr. Inoue wasn't supporting her opinion on the news program yesterday. （例文 5）

_____

(5) The camera crew has been busy since this morning. （例文 10）

_____

(6) According to the TV, many people are evacuating from the unsafe area. （例文 1）

_____

(7) Is she looking for vacant apartment information on the bulletin board? （例文 3）

_____

(8) Was the commentator explaining about the matter in detail? （例文 6）

_____

英文構造把握問題　基礎問題　発展問題　文章理解問題

2. 次の[ ]内の語 (句) を並べ替えて、時制を意識しながら日本文の意味に合う英文を作りなさい。
ただし、文頭の語も小文字にしてあります。

(1) 私は今、卒業論文のための情報収集はしていません。（例文 2）
[collecting / for / graduation / I'm / information / my / not] thesis now.

_____

(2) 私はその悲惨な地震のニュースをスマホで読んでいました。（例文 4）
I [about / the disastrous / earthquake / the news / on / reading / was] my smartphone.

_____

(3) 私は過去に出版社でアルバイトをしたことがある。（例文 7）
[company / for / have / I / part-time / a publishing / worked] in the past.

_____

(4) 私は先週からずっとプレゼン資料の準備をし続けている。（例文 12）
[been / have / I / materials / preparing / presentation / since] last week.

_____

(5) あなたは昨夜、オリンピックの開会式を見ていましたか？（例文 6）
[ceremony / of / opening / the / watching / were / you] the Olympics last night?

_____

(6) あなたはかつてマスコミに関する雑誌記事を読んだことがありますか？（例文 9）
[about / article / ever / have / a magazine / read / you] mass communication?

_____

(7) 昨日、彼は学校新聞の記事を書いてはいませんでした。（例文 5）
[the article / for / he / newspaper / the school / wasn't / writing] yesterday.

_____

(8) アヤはインターネットで安価な留学プログラムを探していますか？（例文 3）
[Aya / for / inexpensive / is / programs / searching / study-abroad] on the internet?

_____

3. 次の [ ] 内の語(句)を並べ替えて、時制を意識しながら日本文の意味に合う英文を作りなさい。
ただし、文頭の語も小文字にしてあります。

(1) 私は以前、ネット断食のイベントに参加したことがある。（例文 7）

I [an event / fasting / for / have / in / internet / participated] before.

_____

(2) 私はあの報道記者がテレビで微笑むのを一度も見たことがない。（例文 8）

I [have / never / news reporter / on / seen / smile / that] TV.

_____

(3) 私は 15 年以上、そのテレビスタジオの近くに住んでいる。（例文 10）

I [for / have / lived / more / near / studio / the TV] than fifteen years.

_____

(4) あなたはもう授業の登録情報を受け取りましたか？（例文 11）

[already / the course / have / information / received / registration / you]?

_____

(5) その当時、日本のほとんど全ての人たちがマスクをつけていた。（例文 4）

Almost [all / in / Japan / people / the / wearing / were] masks in those days.

_____

(6) そのラジオ放送局は現在、その重要なニュースを私たちに報道していません。（例文 2）

The [the important / isn't / news / radio / reporting / station / us] right now.

_____

(7) 最近、日本では不動産価格が急激に上昇してきている。（例文 12）

Recently, [been / estate / have / in / prices / real / rising drastically] Japan.

_____

(8) ソーシャルメディアの発展で世界はますます小さくなっている。（例文 1）

The [because / the development / getting / is / of / smaller / world] of social
media.

_____

英文構造把握問題 基礎問題 発展問題 文章理解問題

4. 次の英文を読み、（1）〜（4）の下線部の語（句）を並べ替えて、意味の通る英文を作りなさい。
ただし、文頭の語も小文字にしてあります。

Reading the News

(1)[bought / ever / have / a news / a newspaper / or / you] magazine? Yesterday, I was listening to an interesting radio program. According to the presenter, more and more (2)[are / Japanese / the news / on / people / reading / their smartphones] instead of buying a newspaper. Until a few decades ago, we could see newspaper salesmen running around neighborhoods in April, knocking on doors, eagerly trying to get people to buy their newspapers. They would offer gifts like boxes of soap powder, beer coupons, and free tickets for museums and art exhibitions. Early morning commuter trains were full of people reading newspapers. These busy office (3)[catch / to / trying / up / were / with / workers] the latest domestic and international events. Tired businessmen would read sports newspapers or evening editions on the same trains home in the evening. Nowadays, however, we rarely see anyone reading a newspaper or a magazine on a train. Most commuters seem to prefer playing games or watching video clips on their smartphones. So, probably, over the past few years, many Japanese (4)[been / have / less / people / reading / spending / time] newspapers and magazines.

(1)　[bought / ever / have / a news / a newspaper / or / you]

_____

(2)　[are / Japanese / the news / on / people / reading / their smartphones]

_____

(3)　[catch / to / trying / up / were / with / workers]

_____

(4)　[been / have / less / people / reading / spending / time]

_____

unit 4 助動詞

トピック 旅行、観光

❚❚❚ 解説 ❚❚❚

　Unit 4では助動詞を扱います。助動詞は動詞の前に付いて、動詞に様々なニュアンスを与えます。基本例文では、助動詞と動詞に下線が引かれているので、動詞のまとまりとして捉えるようにしましょう。また助動詞の文でも、平叙文（肯定文・否定文）や疑問文を作る際のルールを意識化してください。尚、ここでは"have to"という慣用表現も助動詞的な働きをするものとして扱っています。

◀)) 5　 基本例文

can：肯定文

1.　We <u>can sleep</u> in the train during our trip around Europe.
　　ヨーロッパ周遊の旅行中、私たちは電車の中で寝ることができる。

can：否定文

2.　I <u>can't make</u> detailed plans for a trip by myself.
　　私は自分一人では旅行の詳細な計画を立てることができない。

can：疑問文

3.　<u>Can</u> you <u>arrange</u> a five-day trip to Hawaii?
　　5日間のハワイ旅行の手配をしてもらえますか？

could：肯定文・否定文

4.　I <u>could enjoy</u> sightseeing in Shikoku by bicycle.
　　私は自転車で四国観光を楽しむことができた。
　　*否定文：couldn't

could：疑問文

5.　<u>Could</u> you <u>tell</u> me about your travel plans to Mexico?
　　メキシコの旅行プランについて私に教えていただけますか？

will：肯定文・否定文・疑問文

6. Suzuka <u>will be</u> a first-class tour conductor someday.

スズカはいつか一流のツアーコンダクターになるだろう。

*否定文：won't *疑問文：will を文頭に移動

must：肯定文・否定文・疑問文

7. You <u>must be careful</u> during your trip to the mountainous regions.

あなたは山岳地帯への旅行中は注意しなくてはなりません。

*否定文：mustn't（～してはならない） *疑問文：must を文頭に移動

have to：肯定文・否定文・疑問文

8. You <u>have to rush</u> to the airport by taxi.

あなたはタクシーで空港に急いで行かなくてはなりません。

*主語が三人称単数現在→has to

*否定文：(don't / doesn't) have to（～する必要はない）

*疑問文：(Do / Does) ＋主語＋ have to

may：肯定文・否定文・疑問文

9. You <u>may take a trip</u> somewhere by yourself.

あなたは一人でどこかに旅行に行ってもいいですよ。

*否定文：may not *疑問文：may を文頭に移動

*may には「～かもしれない」という意味もあります。

*take a trip は熟語としてまとめて下線が引かれています。

might：肯定文・否定文・疑問文

10. I <u>might go hiking</u> to Mt. Takao this weekend.

*否定文：might not *疑問文：might を文頭に移動

私は今週末、高尾山にハイキングに行くかもしれない。

*go hiking は慣用表現としてまとめて下線が引かれています。

should：肯定文・否定文・疑問文

11. You <u>should go</u> to the Japanese embassy as soon as possible.

あなたはできるだけ早く日本大使館に行くべきです。

*否定文：shouldn't *疑問文：should を文頭に移動

shall：疑問文

12. <u>Shall</u> we <u>stay</u> at this hotel tonight?

今晩は、このホテルに泊まりましょうか?

1. 次の英文の主語に続く動詞（動詞のまとまり）に下線を引き、助動詞を意識しながら意味を言いなさい。

(1)　Can I travel around Kyushu on my bike during this summer vacation?　(例文 3)

(2)　May I have some sightseeing brochures for South East Asia?　(例文 9)

(3)　We couldn't buy souvenirs at the airport due to the tight schedule.　(例文 4)

(4)　We won't arrive in Hakone before noon because of Tetsuya's delay.　(例文 6)

(5)　Do we have to study more about the country before our trip?　(例文 8)

(6)　You can talk with local people in the village during the tour.　(例文 1)

(7)　You mustn't leave your passport in your suitcase during the trip.　(例文 7)

(8)　You shouldn't miss the local food at the roadside stalls.　(例文 11)

英文構造把握問題 | 基礎問題 | 発展問題 | 文章理解問題

2. 次の[ ]内の語 (句) を並べ替えて、助動詞を意識しながら日本文の意味に合う英文を作りなさい。ただし、文頭の語も小文字にしてあります。

(1) 私は今回、福岡に飛行機では行かないかもしれない。（例文 10）

[by / Fukuoka / go / I / might / not / to] airplane this time.

_____

(2) 駅近くの大きくて居心地の良いホテルに泊まってもよいですか？（例文 9）

[at / comfortable / hotel / I / the large / may / stay] near the station?

_____

(3) もう一度、沖縄旅行の計画について話し合いましょうか？（例文 12）

[discuss / for / our / the plan / shall / trip / we] to Okinawa again?

_____

(4) この旅行案内書でその島に関する必要な情報を得ることができますよ。（例文 1）

[about / can / get / information / the island / the necessary / you] from this guidebook.

_____

(5) あなたは 1 日で京都の史跡全てを見ることはできません。（例文 2）

[all / can't / the historical / in / see / spots / you] Kyoto in one day.

_____

(6) あなたは明日の朝、早く家を出る必要はありません。（例文 8）

[don't / early / have / home / leave / to / you] tomorrow morning.

_____

(7) あなたはホテルから空港へはタクシーに乗らなくてはなりません。（例文 7）

[from / the hotel / must / take / a taxi / to / you] the airport.

_____

(8) 神社の前で私たちの写真を撮っていただけますか？（例文 5）

[could / in / of / a picture / take / us / you] front of the shrine?

_____

3. 次の [　] 内の語(句)を並べ替えて、助動詞を意識しながら日本文の意味に合う英文を作りなさい。ただし、文頭の語も小文字にしてあります。

(1) 私は大英博物館で有名な芸術品をたくさん見ることができた。（例文 4）

I [of art / could / famous / in / many / see / works] the British Museum.

_____

(2) 私はこの冬、人生で初めて海外旅行をするかもしれない。（例文 10）

I [abroad / the first / for / in / might / time / travel] my life this winter.

_____

(3) 次の旅行のためにインターネットで航空券を取ってあげましょうか？（例文 12）

[an airline / get / I / on / shall / ticket / you] the internet for your next trip?

_____

(4) 私たちはハネムーン中にそのホテルの最高級の一室に泊まるだろう。（例文 6）

We [the best / in / of / one / rooms / stay / will] at the hotel during our honeymoon.

_____

(5) あなたは電車でも車でもその秘境を訪れることはできません。（例文 2）

[by / can't / regions / train / the unexplored / visit / you] nor by car.

_____

(6) あなたはその村のまだ知られていない景勝地を訪れるべきです。（例文 11）

You [in / scenic / should / spots / the / unknown / visit] the village.

_____

(7) マルタ旅行のために、このガイドブックを貸してもらえますか？（例文 3）

[can / for / guidebook / lend / me / this / you] my trip to Malta?

_____

(8) 一番近い駅までの道を案内していただけますか？（例文 5）

[could / the nearest / show / to / us / the way / you] station?

_____

4. 次の英文を読み、(1) 〜 (4) の下線部の語 (句) を並べ替えて、意味の通る英文を作りなさい。
　 ただし、文頭の語も小文字にしてあります。

Tokyo Disneyland

　　Disneyland is one of the most popular tourist attractions in Tokyo. This amusement park contains around 40 attractions, so (1)[all / cannot / experience / in / one / the rides / you] day. However, to save time, you might want to think about buying a Fastpass. With this pass, you can enter certain attractions quickly (2)[and / do / have / line / not / to / up]. You might want to try the fun roller coaster ride, Big Thunder Mountain. You ride a train through an old mine and drop into canyons. You will also enter dark tunnels and here, the ride can get very bumpy. You may get hungry after running around many attractions. (3)[could / drop / into / the many / of / one / you] restaurants and find many Disney-themed dishes. After lunch, it might be a good idea to stay off the rides. Instead, you could choose to meet Mickey Mouse and his friends or sit down and watch one of the parades. At the end of a long and exciting day, (4)[buy / forget / must / not / some / to / you] souvenirs. You will find shops near the main entrance, and you can buy various goods, including T-shirts, caps, and key rings.

(1)　[all / cannot / experience / in / one / the rides / you]

_____

(2)　[and / do / have / line / not / to / up]

_____

(3)　[could / drop / into / the many / of / one / you]

_____

(4)　[buy / forget / must / not / some / to / you]

_____

unit 5

比較、受け身

トピック 知人、友人

||| 解説 |||

Unit 5では、比較と受け身の文を作る練習をします。比較では「be動詞＋形容詞」、「一般動詞＋副詞」、「be動詞／一般動詞＋形容詞＋名詞」の3つのパターンを練習します。動詞が形容詞・副詞・名詞とどう結びつくのかを意識しながら、原級、比較級、最上級の文の規則性をマスターしましょう。受け身の文法でも動詞のまとまりに着目して、その規則性を意識化しながら英文を作るようにしましょう。

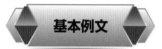

🔊 6　基本例文

原級を使った比較の構文

主語＋be動詞＋as 形容詞 as

1. Daiki is as funny as Akira.
   ダイキはアキラと同じくらい面白い。

主語＋一般動詞＋as 副詞 as

2. Azumi can run as fast as Naomi.
   アズミはナオミと同じくらい速く走ることができる。

主語＋一般動詞＋〜times＋as 形容詞＋名詞 as

3. Mai has three times as many pairs of jeans as Keiko.
   マイはケイコの3倍多くのジーンズを持っている。

   ＊主語＋be動詞＋〜times＋as形容詞asというパターンもあります。

比較級を使った比較の構文

主語＋be動詞＋形容詞 er＋than

4. Kazuya is cleverer than Masaki.
   カズヤはマサキより頭が良い。

主語 + 一般動詞 + 副詞 er + than

5. Miki always <u>gets up</u> earlier than Maki.

ミキはいつもマキより早く<u>起きる</u>。

*gets up は熟語としてまとめて下線が引かれています。

主語 + be動詞 + more 形容詞 + than

6. Karen <u>is</u> more <u>cheerful</u> than anybody else in my team.

私のチームではカレンは他の誰よりも<u>陽気だ</u>。

最上級を使った比較の構文

主語 + be動詞 + the 形容詞 est + 名詞

7. Kanna <u>is</u> the cutest girl among all the group members.

カンナはそのグループメンバー全員の中で一番かわいい女の子<u>だ</u>。

主語 + be動詞 + the most 形容詞 + 名詞

8. Sonta <u>was</u> the most intelligent student in my high school.

ソンタは私の高校では一番頭がいい生徒<u>だった</u>。

主語 + be動詞 + one of the most 形容詞 + 名詞

9. Kayo <u>is</u> one of the most fluent speakers of English in my university.

カヨは私の大学では最も流暢に英語を話す人の一人<u>だ</u>。

*形容詞が短い場合は "one of the 形容詞 est" となります。

受け身

主語 + be動詞 + 過去分詞（SVO の受け身）

10. Yuki <u>is loved</u> by everybody at her workplace.

ユキは職場ではみんなに<u>愛されている</u>。

主語 + be動詞 + 過去分詞（SVOC の受け身）

11. Rieko <u>was called</u> Rick by her American friends.

リエコはアメリカ人の友だちにリックと<u>呼ばれていた</u>。

主語 + 助動詞 + be + 過去分詞

12. Ken <u>will be praised</u> by his homeroom teacher tomorrow.

ケンは明日、担任の先生に<u>褒められるだろう</u>。

1. 次の英文の主語に続く動詞（動詞のまとまり）に下線を引き、比較や受け身を意識しながら意
　 味を言いなさい。

(1) Keita is one of the most aggressive rugby players in the team. （例文 9）

_____

(2) Mutsumi is the most prominent person in the field of e-sports. （例文 8）

_____

(3) Tomo will be met by his host parents at the airport tomorrow. （例文 12）

_____

(4) Toshiki was scolded severely by his homeroom teacher. （例文 10）

_____

(5) No one is more honest than Naoko among my friends. （例文 6）

_____

(6) Nobody is as shy as Kiyoshi among my acquaintances. （例文 1）

_____

(7) Is Yutaka the youngest boy in the heavy rock band? （例文 7）

_____

(8) Does Yuika travel to Korea as often as her mother? （例文 2）

_____

2. 次の [ ]内の語 (句) を並べ替えて、比較や受け身を意識しながら日本文の意味に合う英文を作りなさい。ただし、文頭の語も小文字にしてあります。

(1) その赤ちゃんは日本の歴史上の人物にちなんでヨリトモと名づけられた。（例文 11）

The [after / baby / historic / the Japanese / named / was / Yoritomo] character.

_____

(2) アキコはカラオケボックスで友だちよりも大声で歌を歌った。（例文 5）

[Akiko / her friends / in / louder / sang / songs / than] the karaoke box.

_____

(3) ケメコはマイコの4倍も多くの水を飲む。（例文 3）

[as / drinks / four / Kemeko / much / times / water] as Maiko.

_____

(4) ナオキはそのジムでは一番強いヘビー級のボクサーだ。（例文 7）

[boxer / heavyweight / in / is / Naoki / strongest / the] the gym.

_____

(5) シュンはそのクラブでは最も楽観的なテニス選手だった。（例文 8）

[most / optimistic / player / Shun / tennis / the / was] in the club.

_____

(6) 私のクラスでは、誰もエリカほど怠惰ではない。（例文 1）

[as / as Erika / in / is / lazy / no / one] my class.

_____

(7) 英語部にマジコよりも真面目な人は誰かいますか？（例文 6）

[anybody / in / is / Majiko / more / serious / than] the English club?

_____

(8) あなたの大学でヒデキより賢い人は誰かいますか？（例文 4）

[anybody / Hideki / in / is / than / wiser / your] college?

_____

3. 次の [ ]内の語(句)を並べ替えて、比較や受け身を意識しながら日本文の意味に合う英文を作りなさい。ただし、文頭の語も小文字にしてあります。

(1) その赤ちゃんは生まれた日にちなんで、ヒナと名づけられるべきだ。(例文 12)

The baby [after / be / the day / Hina / named / of / should] her birth.

_____

(2) エイイチは明治時代のパイオニアとして日本人に尊敬されている。(例文 10)

Eiichi [as / by / is / Japanese / people / a pioneer / respected] during the Meiji era.

_____

(3) ケンタはその野性的な性格から「ウルフ」とあだ名をつけられた。(例文 11)

Kenta [because / his / nicknamed / of / was / wild / 'Wolf'] character.

_____

(4) ブンタは大阪で最も有名なお笑い芸人の一人かもしれない。(例文 9)

Bunta [be / famous / might / most / of / one / the] comedians in Osaka.

_____

(5) 私の高校では誰もエイタより速く泳げなかった。(例文 5)

[could / Eita / faster / no / one / swim / than] in my high school.

_____

(6) クラスの誰も僕のガールフレンドほどかわいくはない。(例文 4)

No [class / in / is / my / one / prettier / than] my girlfriend.

_____

(7) トモヨは先生と同じくらい流暢に英語を話すことができますか？(例文 2)

[as / can / English / fluently / as her / speak / Tomoyo] teacher?

_____

(8) ミチの仕事の収入は私より3倍も多い。(例文 3)

Michi's [are / as / earnings / from / her job / three / times] much as mine.

_____

4.　次の英文を読み、(1) ～ (4) の下線部の語 (句) を並べ替えて、意味の通る英文を作りなさい。
　　ただし、文頭の語も小文字にしてあります。

Class Picture

　　Here is a picture of my high school class. (1)[at / the end / our graduation / it / of / taken / was] trip to Vancouver. This is me in the center of the picture. I'm standing next to Keiko; she was my best friend. She was also the most attractive girl in the school. Next to her is Ayaka. (2)[Ayaka / girl / in / intelligent / most / the / was] our class and was chosen by the teacher to be class leader three years in a row. Behind me is Jun. He was taller than me but not as tall as this boy, Kenta in the back row. Kenta (3)[and / class / in / our / tallest / the / was] the captain of the school baseball team. He was the most popular boy in the school and was liked by everyone. In the front row are Saya, Yuri, and Mio. They were close friends and were always hanging out together. They enjoyed studying English, and (4)[best / considered / English / speaker / the / was / Yuri] in our class.

(1)　[at / the end / our graduation / it / of / taken / was]

_____

(2)　[Ayaka / girl / in / intelligent / most / the / was]

_____

(3)　[and / class / in / our / tallest / the / was]

_____

(4)　[best / considered / English / speaker / the / was / Yuri]

_____

unit 6 疑問文 （5W1H, which）

トピック ▶ 家庭、家族

‖ 解説 ‖

　Unit 6 では、5W1H「いつ（when）・どこで（where）・誰が（who）・何を（what）・なぜ（why）・どのように（how）」とwhich（どちら）の 7 つの疑問詞を使った疑問文の作文練習をします。これらの疑問文も be 動詞と一般動詞で作り方が異なるので、Unit 1, 2 で学習した基本をしっかり意識しながら練習してみてください。WH の疑問文は、知らないことをお互いが知るためのツールとして重要な役割を持ち、日常会話でも頻繁に使う文法なので、その規則性をしっかりマスターしましょう。

◀》7  基本例文

`when`

`be動詞の疑問文`

1　When <u>is</u> your younger brother's birthday party?
　　　弟さんの誕生日会はいつ<u>ですか</u>？

`一般動詞の疑問文`

2.　When <u>does</u> your father usually <u>take a bath</u>?
　　　あなたのお父さんはいつもいつ<u>お風呂に入ります</u>か？
　　　*take a bath は熟語としてまとめて下線が引かれています。

`where`

`be動詞の疑問文`

3.　Where <u>is</u> your elder brother's favorite place at home?
　　　家でお兄さんのお気に入りの場所はどこ<u>ですか</u>？

`一般動詞の疑問文`

4.　Where <u>does</u> your family often <u>go</u> for dinner together?
　　　ご家族は夕食をどこによく一緒に食べに<u>行きますか</u>？

who

be動詞/一般動詞の疑問文（whoが主語/補語）

5. Who <u>is</u> the most diligent person in your family?

あなたの家族で誰が一番勤勉な人ですか？

一般動詞の疑問文（whoが目的語）

6. Who <u>does</u> your younger sister <u>like</u> the most among young comedians?

妹さんは若手芸人の中では誰が一番好きですか？

*whoと同様にwhomも使われます。

whose ＋名詞

be動詞/一般動詞の疑問文

7. Whose smartphone <u>is</u> the most expensive in your family?

あなたの家族では誰のスマホが一番高価ですか？

what / what ＋名詞

be動詞の疑問文

8. What <u>is</u> the most popular TV program in your house?

あなたの家で最も人気のあるテレビ番組は何ですか？

一般動詞の疑問文

9. What food <u>does</u> your family <u>eat</u> on New Year's Day?

あなたのご家族はお正月にどんな料理を食べますか？

why

be動詞/一般動詞の疑問文

10. Why <u>is</u> your mother so <u>good</u> at cooking?

あなたのお母さんはなぜ料理がそんなに上手なのですか？

how/how ＋副詞・形容詞 / how many (much) ＋名詞

be動詞 / 一般動詞の疑問文

11. How long <u>does</u> your elder brother usually <u>study</u> at home?

お兄さんはいつも家でどのくらい長く勉強しますか？

which / which ＋名詞

be動詞 / 一般動詞の疑問文

12. Which <u>does</u> your younger brother <u>prefer</u>, baseball or soccer?

弟さんは野球とサッカーではどちらが好きですか？

1. 次の英文の主語に続く動詞（動詞のまとまり）に下線を引き、疑問文（5W1H, which）を意識
   しながら意味を言いなさい。

(1) Why can't we go to grandma's house for our summer vacation? (例文 10)

_____

(2) Whose permission do you need for staying out late at night? (例文 7)

_____

(3) How many years have you had your pet dog? (例文 11)

_____

(4) Who does your elder brother respect the most among his peers? (例文 6)

_____

(5) What time does your father usually come home? (例文 9)

_____

(6) Where is your younger sister's favorite restaurant in the neighborhood? (例文 3)

_____

(7) What are your family's rules about helping out at home? (例文 8)

_____

(8) When is your parents' 20th wedding anniversary? (例文 1)

_____

英文構造把握問題　基礎問題　発展問題　文章理解問題

2. 次の [ ]内の語 (句) を並べ替えて、疑問文 (5W1H, which) を意識しながら日本文の意味に合う英文を作りなさい。ただし、文頭の語も小文字にしてあります。

(1) カーテンは、ピンクと緑ではどちらの色を選びますか？（例文 12）

[choose / color / for / the / which / will / you] curtains, pink or green?

_____

(2) あなたは昨夜、家族と何のゲームをしましたか？（例文 9）

[did / games / play / what / with / you / your] family last night?

_____

(3) あなたの家族では誰がいつもペットの猫の世話をするのですか？（例文 5）

[always / care / of / pet cat / takes / the / who] in your family?

_____

(4) あなたのお父さんは市長候補の中で誰を選ぶのでしょうか？（例文 6）

[among / the candidates / choose / father / who / will / your] for mayor?

_____

(5) あなたのお母さんは週末、どこによくハイキングに行きますか？（例文 4）

[does / go / hiking / mother / often / where / your] at weekends?

_____

(6) あなたのおじさんはいつ、山にログハウスを建てたのですか？（例文 2）

[build / did / his / log cabin / uncle / when / your] in the mountains?

_____

(7) あなたのお母さんの好きなイタリア料理と飲み物は何ですか？（例文 8）

[dish / favorite / is / Italian / mother's / what / your] and drink?

_____

(8) お兄さんの次のライブ演奏はいつですか？（例文 1）

[brother's / elder / is / live / next / when / your] performance?

_____

3. 次の [ ] 内の語(句)を並べ替えて、疑問文 (5W1H, which) を意識しながら日本文の意味に合う英文を作りなさい。ただし、文頭の語も小文字にしてあります。

(1) 両親へのサプライズパーティーをいつ開きましょうか？ （例文 2）

[for / hold / party / shall / the surprise / we / when] our parents?

_____

(2) あなたは家族の中では誰のアドバイスに一番耳を傾けますか？ （例文 7）

[advice / do / listen / the most / to / whose / you] in your family?

_____

(3) あなたは何日間、おじさんの別荘に泊まる予定ですか？ （例文 11）

[are / days / going / how / many / to / you] stay at your uncle's cottage?

_____

(4) あなたの家族では誰が一番おしゃべりな人ですか？ （例文 5）

[in / is / most / person / talkative / the / who] your family?

_____

(5) あなたのおじいちゃんは朝、どこでよく散歩しますか？ （例文 4）

[does / grandpa / often / take / a walk / where / your] in the morning?

_____

(6) なぜ学童保育は彼にとって家庭のようなものなのだろうか？ （例文 10）

[after-school / center / childcare / is / like / the / why] home for him?

_____

(7) 兄の結婚披露宴に一番良い場所はどこでしょうか？ （例文 3）

[be / best / for / place / the / where / would] my elder brother's wedding reception?

_____

(8) 三鷹と吉祥寺では、どちらがあなたの家に一番近い駅ですか？ （例文 12）

[house / is / nearest / station to / the / which / your], Mitaka or Kichijoji?

_____

4. 次の英文を読み、(1) ～ (4) の下線部の語 (句) を並べ替えて、意味の通る英文を作りなさい。
　　ただし、文頭の語も小文字にしてあります。

Family Time

　　(1)[do / how / much / spend / time / with / you] your family? According to a recent survey in the United States, American adults spent, on average, three hours per day on social media but only about 40 minutes of quality time together with their families on the weekdays. Japanese fathers spend many hours at work or work away from home, while mothers look after the children. This is the traditional image of a Japanese family. However, times have changed, and an increasing number of fathers now spend more time at home and less time in the office. In addition, more Japanese mothers are working full-time, and their children spend more time at school, participating in after-school activities, and attending cram school. So, (2)[can / families / how / Japanese / much / spend / time] together, and what can they do together? (3)[do / family / member / most / spend / which / you] of your time with? (4)[do / how / like / spend / time / to / you] with your family? Do you want to spend more time doing things with your mother, father, and siblings?

(1)　[do / how / much / spend / time / with / you]

_____

(2)　[can / families / how / Japanese / much / spend / time]

_____

(3)　[do / family / member / most / spend / which / you]

_____

(4)　[do / how / like / spend / time / to / you]

_____

復習問題

(Unit 1 ～ 6)

1. Unit 1 の例文を参考に、次の [ ] 内の語 (句) を並べ替えて、文型を意識しながら日本文の意味に合う英文を作りなさい。ただし、文頭の語も小文字にしてあります。尚、以下の問題で扱っているトピックは「旅行、観光」になります。

(1) 私はミナミがネットで電車の座席を予約しているのを見た。(例文 12)

[I / Minami / on / reserving / saw / seat / a train] the internet.

_____

(2) 私たちは通りの露店で様々な地元の料理を食べた。(例文 7)

We [at / ate / foods / local / open-air / stalls / various] on the street.

_____

(3) 私たちはその陽気なツアーコンダクターをハナちゃんと呼んだ。(例文 10)

[called / cheerful / conductor / Hana-chan / the / tour / we].

_____

(4) 私たちは昨夜、居心地の良いホテルに泊まった。(例文 3)

[a / at / cozy / hotel / last / stayed / we] night.

_____

(5) 彼は私に沖縄旅行のための素晴らしい本を買ってくれた。(例文 8)

He [book / bought / for / me / to / traveling / a wonderful] Okinawa.

_____

(6) その南国の島には美しいビーチがたくさんある。(例文 2)

There [tropical / beaches / beautiful / many / on / the / are] island.

_____

(7) 海外旅行はいつも私をわくわくさせ、気分転換させてくれる。(例文 9)

[abroad / always / excited / makes / me / and refreshed / traveling].

_____

(8) 彼女のスーツケースはいつもたくさんの服で一杯だ。(例文 5)

Her [always / clothes / full / is / a lot of / suitcase / with].

_____

2. Unit 2 の例文を参考に、次の [　] 内の語 (句) を並べ替えて、時制を意識しながら日本文の意味に合う英文を作りなさい。ただし、文頭の語も小文字にしてあります。尚、以下の問題で扱っているトピックは「知人、友人」になります。

(1) 私はユリコのキャリアプランについて何も知らない。（例文 6）

I [about / anything / career / don't / know / plan / Yuriko's].

_____

(2) ヒサシの結婚のプランについて何か知っていますか？（例文 7）

[about / anything / do / Hisashi's / know / wedding / you] plans?

_____

(3) この写真の少年は私の親友の一人です。（例文 3）

The [boy / in / is / of / one / photo / this] my best friends.

_____

(4) ノリオは高校時代、とても活発だった。（例文 4）

[active / high / his / in / Norio / very / was] school days.

_____

(5) カズミは気に入っている会社のインターンシップに応募した。（例文 10）

Kazumi [applied / company's / favorite / for / her / internship / program].

_____

(6) マサコは今年の夏、ニュージーランドの友だちを訪ねる予定だ。（例文 12）

Masako [friend / going / her / in / is / to / visit] New Zealand this summer.

_____

(7) ヤスはいつもすぐにあなたのメールに返事をしますか？（例文 9）

[always / does / e-mail / respond / to / Yasu / your] quickly?

_____

(8) ヒロは締切までに宿題を提出しましたか？（例文 11）

[the assignment / by / did / due / Hiro / submit / the] date?

_____

3. Unit 3の例文を参考に、次の［　］内の語（句）を並べ替えて、時制を意識しながら日本文の意味に合う英文を作りなさい。ただし、文頭の語も小文字にしてあります。尚、以下の問題で扱っているトピックは「家庭、家族」になります。

(1) 弟は以前、仙台に自転車で旅したことがある。（例文 7）

My [brother / by / has / Sendai / to / traveled / younger] bicycle before.

_____

(2) お父さんは今、庭で野菜を植えている。（例文 1）

[dad / the garden / in / is / my / planting / vegetables] now.

_____

(3) おばあちゃんは2時間ずっとコンピュータゲームをやり続けている。（例文 12）

My [been / computer / for / games / grandma / has / playing] two hours.

_____

(4) おじいちゃんはちょうど歩行運動を終えたところだ。（例文 11）

[finished / grandpa / has / his / just / my / walking] exercise.

_____

(5) ママは昨日の今頃、カフェで友だちとおしゃべりしていた。（例文 4）

[at / chatting / her friends / mom / my / was / with] a cafe this time yesterday.

_____

(6) 妹は2年間、大学の寮に住んでいる。（例文 10）

My younger [dormitory / for / has / in / lived / sister / the university] two years.

_____

(7) あなたのお姉さんは今、テレビでサッカーの試合を見ていますか？（例文 3）

[elder / is / match / sister / a soccer / watching / your] on TV now?

_____

(8) あなたのおじさんは以前、あの有名なイタリア料理屋で働いていたことがありますか？（例文 9）

[famous / for / has / that / uncle / worked / your] Italian restaurant before?

_____

英文構造把握問題　基礎問題　発展問題　文章理解問題　復習問題

4. Unit 4 の例文を参考に、次の [ ] 内の語 (句) を並べ替えて、助動詞を意識しながら日本文の意味に合う英文を作りなさい。ただし、文頭の語も小文字にしてあります。尚、以下の問題で扱っているトピックは「気候、季節」になります。

(1) 私は雨の日には自転車で学校に行くことができない。（例文 2）

I [bicycle / by / can't / go / on / school / to] rainy days.

_____

(2) こんな寒い冬の日には家にいてもいいですか？（例文 9）

[a / home / I / may / on / stay / such] cold winter day?

_____

(3) この地域では夜、たくさん流れ星を見ることができますよ。（例文 1）

You [at / can / many / night / see / shooting / stars] in this region.

_____

(4) こんな嵐の日にはあなたは家にいなくてはなりません。（例文 8）

You [have / home / on / to / stay / a stormy / such] day.

_____

(5) 梅雨の間、あなたは毎日傘を持っていかなければなりません。（例文 7）

You [an / day / during / every / must / take / umbrella] the rainy season.

_____

(6) こんな気持のいい日には散歩をするべきだ。（例文 11）

[in / lovely / should / such / take / a walk / you] weather.

_____

(7) 悪天候のため彼女は友だちとテニスをすることができなかった。（例文 4）

She [because / couldn't / her friends / of / play / tennis / with] the bad weather.

_____

(8) 天気予報によると、明日はとても暑くなるでしょう。（例文 6）

According to [be / forecast, / hot / it / very / the weather / will] tomorrow.

_____

5. Unit 5の例文を参考に、次の[ ]内の語（句）を並べ替えて、比較や受け身を意識しながら日本文の意味に合う英文を作りなさい。ただし、文頭の語も小文字にしてあります。尚、以下の問題で扱っているトピックは「趣味、娯楽」になります。

(1) 私はあなたの3倍も多くの漫画本を持っている。（例文3）

I [as / books / comic / have / many / three / times] as you.

_____

(2) その老婦人は若い男性と同じくらい速くマラソンを走ることができる。（例文2）

The [as / can / fast / marathons / old / run / woman] as young men.

_____

(3) 私の高校では誰もサヤほど上手にテニスをすることはできない。（例文5）

[better / can / no / one / play / tennis / than] Saya in my high school.

_____

(4) クマゴンは日本で最も人気のあるキャラクターの1つだ。（例文9）

Kumagon [characters / is / most / of / one / popular / the] in Japan.

_____

(5) その曲の歌詞は私の妹によって書かれたものです。（例文10）

The lyrics of [by / my / sister / the song / were / written / younger].

_____

(6) このミステリー映画はあのアクション映画より面白い。（例文6）

This mystery movie [action / interesting / is / more / movie / than / that].

_____

(7) 彼女の新曲は多くの若者によって歌われるでしょう。（例文12）

Her new song [be / by / many / people / sung / will / young].

_____

(8) 朝の散歩はヨガの練習と同じくらい爽快だ。（例文1）

[as / are / exercises / morning / refreshing / walks / as yoga].

_____

英文構造把握問題　基礎問題　発展問題　文章理解問題　復習問題

6. Unit 6 の例文を参考に、次の [ ] 内の語（句）を並べ替えて、疑問文（5W1H, which）を意識しながら日本文の意味に合う英文を作りなさい。ただし、文頭の語も小文字にしてあります。尚、以下の問題で扱っているトピックは「ニュース、情報」になります。

(1) いつもどこで朝刊を読みますか？（例文 4）

[do / morning / read / the / usually / where / you] newspaper?

---

(2) TVK と TVC では、どちらのテレビ局がより好きですか？（例文 12）

[better / do / like / station / TV / which / you], TVK or TVC?

---

(3) どのようにして研究プロジェクトの情報を収集したのですか？（例文 11）

[collect / did / for / how / the information / you / your] research project?

---

(4) プレゼンのためにどんな参考文献を読みましたか？（例文 9）

[books / for / have / read / reference / what / you] your presentation?

---

(5) なぜあの広告会社で働きたいのですか？（例文 10）

[do / for / to / want / why / work / you] that advertising company?

---

(6) 地元のテレビ局で好きなニュースキャスターは誰ですか？（例文 5）

[your favorite / from / is / local / newscaster / who / your] TV station?

---

(7) 次の宿題の締切はいつでしょうか？（例文 1）

[date / the due / for / is / next / our / when] assignment?

---

(8) 卒業論文のトピックは何ですか？（例文 8）

[graduation / is / of / thesis / the topic / what / your]?

unit 8 不定詞（名詞的用法）、動名詞、疑問詞など

トピック 健康

‖‖ 解 説 ‖‖

　Unit 8では名詞的な語句のまとまり（名詞句）を含む文に取り組みます。名詞的な語句のまとまりは、多くの場合、Unit 1で学んだ5文型の主要素である主語、補語、目的語のどこかに位置付けられます。基本例文では便宜的に名詞的な語句のまとまりを山かっこでくくることで、それが文のなかでどこに位置するのかをわかりやすくしました。文法項目としては主に不定詞と動名詞、疑問詞＋不定詞なので、それらを含む文が作れるよう、しっかり練習しましょう。

◀)) 8  基本例文

不定詞の名詞的用法

補語：主語＋be動詞＋to -

1.　My motto is <to exercise every morning>.
　　私のモットーは〈毎朝運動すること〉です。

目的語：主語＋一般動詞＋ to -

2.　I forgot <to clean my teeth>.
　　私は〈歯磨きをするの〉を忘れた。

目的語：主語＋tell/ask等＋人＋ to -

3.　My parents often told me <to go to bed early>.
　　両親はよく私に〈早く寝るよう〉言った。

形式主語：It ＋ be動詞＋形容詞＋for人＋to -

4.　It is important for us <to keep our health>.
　　〈健康を保つこと〉は私たちにとって重要だ。

形式主語：It ＋ be動詞＋形容詞（性格）＋of人＋to -

5　It is wise of you <to choose healthy ingredients for every dish>.
　　〈毎回の料理で健康的な食材を選ぶ〉とはあなたは賢明ですね。

動名詞

主語

6. <Gargling and washing your hands> <u>prevents</u> diseases.
〈うがいと手洗い〉は病気を<u>予防してくれる</u>。

補語：主語＋be動詞＋動詞 ing

7. My daily routine <u>is</u> <getting up early in the morning>.
私の日課は〈朝早く起きること〉<u>だ</u>。

目的語：主語＋一般動詞＋動詞 ing

8. I <u>like</u> <taking a walk with my dog>.
私は〈犬と散歩すること〉が<u>好きだ</u>。

疑問詞＋不定詞

(when, where, who, what, how, which) ＋ to -

9. Please <u>let</u> me <u>know</u> <where to find healthy food>.
〈どこで健康食品を見つけたらいいのか〉私に<u>教えてください</u>。
＊「使役動詞と動詞」は本書では「動詞のまとまり」として扱っています。

what＋名詞＋to -

10. I <u>have to decide</u> <what sports to do for my health>.
私は〈健康のためにどんなスポーツをすべきか〉<u>決めなくてはならない</u>。

which＋名詞＋to -

11. He <u>asked</u> me <which vitamin supplement to take>.
彼は〈どのビタミン剤を飲んだらいいのか〉私に<u>聞いた</u>。

接続詞

whether to - or not/whether or not to -

12. She <u>wondered</u> <whether to quit yoga lessons or not>.
彼女は〈ヨガのレッスンを辞めるべきかどうか〉<u>考えた</u>。

1. 次の英文の主語に続く動詞（動詞のまとまり）に下線を引き、名詞的な語句のまとまりを意識
   しながら意味を言いなさい。

(1) I have to think how to keep fit. （例文 9）

_____

(2) Please tell me which non-fattening food to buy. （例文 11）

_____

(3) He was wondering whether or not to stop smoking. （例文 12）

_____

(4) It is essential for you to eat vegetables with each meal. （例文 4）

_____

(5) It is kind of you to give me a massage. （例文 5）

_____

(6) My daily routine is to do 20 sit-ups before bed time. （例文 1）

_____

(7) One of my bad habits is eating too much ramen. （例文 7）

_____

(8) Using a car too much would weaken the strength of your leg muscles. （例文 6）

_____

英文構造把握問題　　基礎問題　　発展問題　　文章理解問題

2. 次の [ ]内の語（句）を並べ替えて、名詞的な語句のまとまりを意識しながら日本文の意味に合う英文を作りなさい。ただし、文頭の語も小文字にしてあります。

(1) 朝食にどのヨーグルトを食べたらいいのか私にはわかりません。（例文 11）

I [don't / eat / for / know / to / which / yogurt] breakfast.

_____

(2) 私はたまに瞑想することに決めた。（例文 2）

[decided / I / in / meditation / once / practice / to] a while.

_____

(3) 咳止め薬をどこで買ったらよいか教えてください。（例文 9）

Please [buy / cough / me / medicine / tell / to / where].

_____

(4) 健康チェックのためにどんなスマホアプリを使ったらいいのか教えてください。（例文 10）

Please tell [app / for / me / smartphone / to / use / what] checking my health.

_____

(5) 凝り固まった筋肉のストレッチはもう終えましたか？（例文 8）

[finished / have / muscles / stretching / tight / you / your]?

_____

(6) コーチはいつも私に毎日牛乳を飲むようアドバイスする。（例文 3）

My coach [advises / always / drink / every / me / milk / to] day.

_____

(7) 私の好きなことは露天風呂の温泉に浸かることです。（例文 1）

My favorite thing [hot / in / is / an open-air / soak / spring / to].

_____

(8) ビールの飲み過ぎは健康に良くない。（例文 6）

[much beer / drinking / for / good / isn't / too / your] health.

_____

3. 次の [　] 内の語(句)を並べ替えて、名詞的な語句のまとまりを意識しながら日本文の意味に合う英文を作りなさい。ただし、文頭の語も小文字にしてあります。

(1) 私はどんなバランスの良い食事を毎日取ったらいいのか考えたことがない。（例文 10）

I've [balanced / considered / diet / eat / never / to / what] every day.

_____

(2) 私は学校に徒歩で通うか自転車で通うか考えなくてはならない。（例文 12）

I must [consider / on foot / go to / or / school / to / whether] by bicycle.

_____

(3) 今晩、私たちのためにベジタリアン料理を作ってもらえませんか？（例文 8）

Do [a / cooking / dish / for / mind / vegetarian / you] us tonight?

_____

(4) 彼は来月末までに血圧を下げることを目標にしている。（例文 2）

He [aims / his blood / by / the end / lower / pressure / to] of next month.

_____

(5) 医者は私に 1 日 30 分の運動を 1 ヶ月間するよう言った。（例文 3）

The doctor [a / exercise / for / me / 30 minutes / to / told] day for one month.

_____

(6) この素敵なスパに私を連れて行ってくれるとはあなたは親切ですね。（例文 5）

It [is / me / nice / of / to take / to / you] this wonderful spa.

_____

(7) 感染症の大流行中にマスクをつけることは私たちにとって不可欠だった。（例文 4）

It [for / indispensable / a mask / to / us / was / wear] during the pandemic.

_____

(8) 私の気晴らしの 1 つは親しい友人と飲んでおしゃべりすることだ。（例文 7）

One [and chatting / drinking / is / my / of / my pastimes / with] close friends.

_____

4. 次の英文を読み、(1) ～ (4) の下線部の語 (句) を並べ替えて、意味の通る英文を作りなさい。
ただし、文頭の語も小文字にしてあります。

A Lifestyle Change

During my yearly health check, (1)[advised / do / doctor / me / more / my / to] exercise. After hearing this, I decided to make some changes to my lifestyle. I started by setting myself some goals. My first aim was to walk 10,000 steps a day. I started to get off the train one station earlier to achieve my daily step count. I also decided to start going to a yoga class at the local gym every week on Saturdays. (2)[at / enjoy / exercising / friends / I / new / with] the gym. Furthermore, my friend told me to check the internet for free exercise videos. (3)[exercises / following / in / is / really / the / the videos] motivating. I enjoy doing the exercises in the morning before work. It (4)[doing / for / important / is / keep / me / to] these new activities, and I decided to make these changes my new normal routine. I hope these changes will make me healthier. Now, my aim is to improve my diet by adding vegetarian meals a few times a week. Why don't you try a lifestyle change, too?

(1)　[advised / do / doctor / me / more / my / to]

_____

(2)　[at / enjoy / exercising / friends / I / new / with]

_____

(3)　[exercises / following / in / is / really / the / the videos]

_____

(4)　[doing / for / important / is / keep / me / to]

_____

unit 9

接続詞 (that, if / whether)、疑問詞

トピック 異性、恋愛

⦀ 解説 ⦀

　Unit 9では名詞的な文のまとまり（名詞節）を含む文に取り組みます。名詞的な語句のまとまりと同様に、文のまとまりも、多くの場合、主語や補語や目的語になります。名詞的な文のまとまりも、基本例文では山かっこでくくり、文中での位置を明確化しました。これまで通り、主文の動詞や動詞のまとまりに下線を引きますが、名詞的な文のまとまりの中にも主語と動詞があるので、こちらの動詞や動詞のまとまりにも下線を引きました。そうすることで、常に主語と動詞のつながりを意識化することができます。

◀)) 9 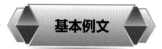 基本例文

接続詞：that節

補語：主語＋ be動詞＋ that -

1. The fact is <that love is blind>.
   事実は、〈愛は盲目だということ〉である。

目的語：主語＋一般動詞＋ that -

2. I think <that Takuya loves you>.
   〈タクヤはあなたが好きだ〉と私は思う。

目的語：主語＋ tell/advise 等＋人＋ that -

3. Kaori advised me <that I should exchange e-mail addresses with him>.
   カオリは私に〈彼とメアドを交換すべきだ〉とアドバイスした。

形容詞の後のthat節：主語＋ be動詞＋形容詞＋ that -

4. I'm surprised <that my boyfriend won the best actor award>.
   私は〈自分のボーイフレンドがベスト男優賞を獲得したこと〉に驚いている。

形式主語：It ＋ be動詞＋形容詞＋ that -

5. It's unbelievable <that the comedian married such a beautiful actress>.
   〈そのお笑い芸人があんな美しい女優と結婚したこと〉は信じられない。

仮定法

I wish ＋主語＋be動詞の過去形（were）-

6. I <u>wish</u> <I <u>were</u> a member of a popular idol group>.
〈私が人気アイドルグループのメンバー<u>だったらなあ</u>〉と<u>思う</u>。
*that節の "that" は省略されています。

I wish ＋ 主語＋一般動詞の過去形 -

7. I <u>wish</u> <I <u>knew</u> her cellphone number>.
〈私が彼女の携帯電話番号を<u>知っていたらなあ</u>〉と<u>思う</u>。
*that節の "that" は省略されています。

疑問詞節

（when, where, who, what, which）＋be動詞 -

8. Please <u>tell</u> me <who <u>is</u> Kenji's girlfriend>.
〈誰がケンジのガールフレンド<u>であるのか</u>〉<u>教えて</u>ください。

（when, where, who, what, why, how, which）＋主語＋一般動詞 -

9. I <u>want to know</u> <where Tsuyoshi <u>lives</u>>.
私は〈ツヨシがどこに<u>住んでいるのか</u>〉知りたい。
*want to という慣用表現は本書では助動詞的な働きをするものとして扱っています。

（what, which）＋名詞＋be動詞/（主語＋）一般動詞 -

10. Nobody <u>told</u> me <what food Fumiya <u>likes</u>>.
〈フミヤがどんな料理が<u>好きなのか</u>〉誰も<u>教えてくれなかった</u>。

how many/much＋名詞＋be動詞/（主語＋）一般動詞 -

11. He <u>didn't tell</u> me <how many love letters he <u>got</u> from Minori>.
彼は〈ミノリから何通ラブレターを<u>もらったのか</u>〉私に<u>教えてくれなかった</u>。

接続詞：if/whether

補語/目的語：主語＋be動詞/一般動詞＋if/whether -

12. I <u>wonder</u> <if Mamiko <u>has</u> a steady boyfriend>.
私は〈マミコに決まったボーイフレンドが<u>いるのかどうか</u>〉と思う。
*マミコには決まったボーイフレンドが<u>いる</u>のだろうか。

1. 次の英文の主語に続く動詞（動詞のまとまり）に下線を引き、名詞的な文のまとまりを意識しながら意味を言いなさい。

(1) I wish I were his favorite type of girl. （例文 6）

_____

(2) I wonder how many rice balls I should make for his lunch. （例文 11）

_____

(3) I want to know if they are living together in that apartment. （例文 12）

_____

(4) I believe that Tomoya will be my prospective marriage partner. （例文 2）

_____

(5) Could you tell me when is a good day for our next date? （例文 8）

_____

(6) Shinji didn't tell me how he met his girlfriend. （例文 9）

_____

(7) It was disappointing that Mariko declined my marriage proposal. （例文 5）

_____

(8) The truth is that first love never lasts forever. （例文 1）

_____

2. 次の[　]内の語（句）を並べ替えて、名詞的な文のまとまりを意識しながら日本文の意味に合う
英文を作りなさい。ただし、文頭の語も小文字にしてあります。

(1) 私は恋人がまだ元カレを愛していることがとても悲しい。（例文 4）

I'm very [ex-boyfriend / my girlfriend / her / loves / sad / still / that].

(2) 私はケイスケがトモコと恋愛したということを疑っている。（例文 2）

I [doubt / fell / in / Keisuke / love / that / with] Tomoko.

(3) 私がサトシと同じクラスだったらなあ。（例文 6）

I [as / class / I / in / the same / were / wish] Satoshi.

(4) ボーイフレンドが私のアパートのもっと近くに住んでいたらなあ。（例文 7）

[my boyfriend / I / lived / my / nearer / to / wish] apartment.

(5) 私はなぜあなたがタカエと別れたのかわからない。（例文 9）

I [broke / don't / know / up / why / with / you] Takae.

(6) 私はアスカがカフェでどんなデザートをよく食べているか知りたい。（例文 10）

I want to [Asuka / at / dessert / eats / know / often / what] the cafe.

(7) トモミは私の彼氏がサキからバレンタインの贈物をもらったと私に告げた。（例文 3）

Tomomi told [my boyfriend / from / gift / got / me / that / a Valentine] Saki.

(8) 私のアドバイスは、あなたが彼との距離を置くべきだということだ。（例文 1）

My advice [away / from / is / should / stay / that / you] him.

3. 次の [　] 内の語(句)を並べ替えて、名詞的な文のまとまりを意識しながら日本文の意味に合う
英文を作りなさい。ただし、文頭の語も小文字にしてあります。

(1) 私はヒナノがメガネをはずしたらとてもキュートに見えたことに驚いた。（例文 4）

I was [cute / Hinano / looked / so / surprised / that / without] her glasses.

_____

(2) タケルのためにおいしいピクニックランチを作ることができたらなあ。（例文 7）

I [could / a delicious / for / I / picnic lunch / make / wish] Takeru.

_____

(3) あなたが私の愛を彼に伝えてくれることができるかしらと思う。（例文 12）

I [could / him / my love / send / whether / wonder / you].

_____

(4) 私はあなたが何回キミコをデートに誘ったのか知りたい。（例文 11）

I want to know [asked / have / how / Kimiko / many / times / you] out for a date.

_____

(5) 私たちはどこが結婚披露宴に最も望ましい場所か考えなくてはならない。（例文 8）

We have [about / is / most / the / think / to / where] desirable place for our
wedding reception.

_____

(6) カナエとのデートのためにどんなプランを立てたらいいか教えましょう。（例文 10）

Let me [for / make / plans / should / tell you / what / you] a date with Kanae.

_____

(7) ユミはトキオからのプロポーズを受け入れるかもしれないと私に言った。（例文 3）

Yumi [accept / the marriage / me / might / she / that / told] proposal from Tokio.

_____

(8) ダイスケがマナミと付き合っているというのは本当だ。（例文 5）

[Daisuke / going / is / it / out / that / is true] with Manami.

_____

英文構造把握問題 　 基礎問題 　 発展問題 　 文章理解問題

4. 次の英文を読み、(1) ～ (4) の下線部の語 (句) を並べ替えて、意味の通る英文を作りなさい。

Valentine's Day

Valentine's Day is a special day in many countries around the world. It is a celebration of love and often a day to give gifts or go on a date with our partners. Do you (1)[about / send / think / a Valentine / who / will / you] card to next February 14? We all (2)[could / from / gift / receive / a special / we / wish] our loved ones. Many people can't wait to see (3)[from / gifts / partners / receive / their / they / what] or secret admirers. In addition, in Japan, many people also spend a lot of time and effort making sweets at home to give to their friends and coworkers. For people from other countries, (4)[give / is / it / Japanese / people / surprising / that] Valentine's gifts to their boss! Valentine's day is also a day to think about the perfect place for a date. It is true that a romantic dinner date is a lovely treat for Valentine's day. You should choose a restaurant with romantic lighting and delicious food. You should find out your partner's favorite food and pick a place famous for that food. We can all wish we were someone's Valentine next February 14.

(1) [about / send / think / a Valentine / who / will / you]

_____

(2) [could / from / gift / receive / a special / we / wish]

_____

(3) [from / gifts / partners / receive / their / they / what]

_____

(4) [give / is / it / Japanese / people / surprising / that]

_____

unit 10 不定詞（副詞的用法）、付帯状況、分詞構文

トピック 仕事、職業

▌▌▌ 解説 ▌▌▌

　Unit 10では、主に動詞を修飾する副詞や副詞的な語句のまとまり（副詞句）を含む文に取り組みます。Unit 1でも説明したように、副詞や副詞的な語句のまとまりは文の主要素にはなりません。基本例文では副詞や副詞的な語句のまとまりを便宜的に丸かっこでくくることで、その位置がわかりやすくなるよう試みました。文法項目としては、主に不定詞、付帯状況、分詞構文を扱うので、それらを含む文が作れるよう、しっかり練習しましょう。

◀》10  基本例文

副詞

副詞（単語）

1. (Recently,) I'm (always) <u>doing</u> my work (carefully).
   （最近）私は（いつも）（注意深く）仕事をしている。

前置詞＋名詞

時

2. Tamami <u>has been absent</u> from work (since last Wednesday).
   タマミは（先週の水曜から）仕事を<u>ずっと休んでいる</u>。

場所

3. I <u>could find</u> a good part-time job (near my house).
   私は（自宅の近くで）良いバイト先を<u>見つけることができた</u>。

その他

4. Yoshiko <u>goes</u> to her part-time job (by train).
   ヨシコは（電車で）バイト先に<u>行く</u>。

56

不定詞の副詞的用法

目的

5. I'm studying English (to become a cabin attendant).

私は（CAになるために）英語を勉強している。

原因・理由

6. My teacher was delighted (to hear my decision about my career choice).

先生は（私の職業選択での決定を聞いて）喜んだ。

判断の根拠：〜するとは/〜するには

7. How careless he was (to make the same mistake again and again)!

（何度も何度も同じミスをするとは）彼はなんと不注意だったのか！

慣用表現：enough to -

8. We were brave enough (to start our own new business).

私たちは（自分たちの新しいビジネスを始めるほど）十分勇気があった。

慣用表現：too〜to -

9. The job training was too hard for me (to complete).

職業研修は私にとって（終えるには）大変過ぎた。

否定

10. I got up early (not to be late for work).

私は（仕事に遅刻しないように）早く起きた。

*got upは熟語としてまとめて下線が引かれています。

付帯状況

with＋名詞＋前置詞句

11. The sales manager approached me (with a smile on her face).

営業部長が（顔に笑みを浮かべて）私に近づいてきた。

分詞構文

〜しながら

12. My colleague is always working at his desk, (drinking coffee).

同僚は、（珈琲を飲みながら）いつも机で仕事をしている。

1. 次の英文の主語に続く動詞（動詞のまとまり）に下線を引き、副詞や副詞的な語句のまとまりを意識しながら意味を言いなさい。

(1) I was disappointed to fail such an important job interview. (例文 6)

_____

(2) I have joined various internships to choose my future occupation. (例文 5)

_____

(3) I have to find a job before graduation. (例文 2)

_____

(4) Let's rewrite our product presentation not to cause confusion. (例文 10)

_____

(5) She was lucky enough to receive a tentative job offer. (例文 8)

_____

(6) She complained about workplace harassment with tears in her eyes. (例文 11)

_____

(7) Suddenly, the part-timer started to work earnestly. (例文 1)

_____

(8) The topic of the group discussion was too difficult for me to cope with. (例文 9)

_____

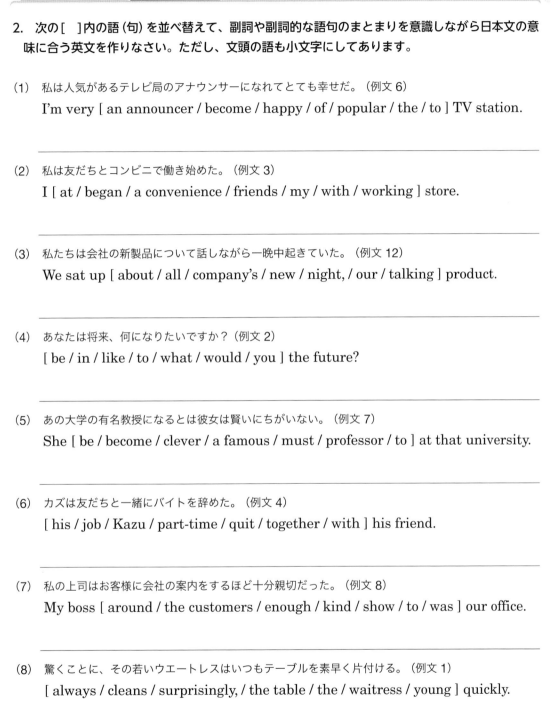

2. 次の[ ]内の語(句)を並べ替えて、副詞や副詞的な語句のまとまりを意識しながら日本文の意味に合う英文を作りなさい。ただし、文頭の語も小文字にしてあります。

(1) 私は人気があるテレビ局のアナウンサーになれてとても幸せだ。(例文6)

I'm very [an announcer / become / happy / of / popular / the / to] TV station.

(2) 私は友だちとコンビニで働き始めた。(例文3)

I [at / began / a convenience / friends / my / with / working] store.

(3) 私たちは会社の新製品について話しながら一晩中起きていた。(例文12)

We sat up [about / all / company's / new / night, / our / talking] product.

(4) あなたは将来、何になりたいですか？(例文2)

[be / in / like / to / what / would / you] the future?

(5) あの大学の有名教授になるとは彼女は賢いにちがいない。(例文7)

She [be / become / clever / a famous / must / professor / to] at that university.

(6) カズは友だちと一緒にバイトを辞めた。(例文4)

[his / job / Kazu / part-time / quit / together / with] his friend.

(7) 私の上司はお客様に会社の案内をするほど十分親切だった。(例文8)

My boss [around / the customers / enough / kind / show / to / was] our office.

(8) 驚くことに、その若いウエートレスはいつもテーブルを素早く片付ける。(例文1)

[always / cleans / surprisingly, / the table / the / waitress / young] quickly.

3. 次の [   ] 内の語(句)を並べ替えて、副詞や副詞的な語句のまとまりを意識しながら日本文の意味に合う英文を作りなさい。ただし、文頭の語も小文字にしてあります。

(1) 私は英語の教員免許を取るためにずっと一生懸命勉強し続けている。（例文 5）

[been / an English / get / hard / I've / studying / to] teaching license.

_____

(2) 私は新しい顧客を探しながら 3 時間ずっと歩き続けている。（例文 12）

I've [been / for / hours, / looking for / new / three / walking] clients.

_____

(3) 私たちは時代遅れにならないように新しい技術を学ばなくてはならない。（例文 10）

[be / have to / learn / not / new technologies / to / we] out of date.

_____

(4) インターンシップ中に、あなたは失敗から多くのことを学ぶことができますよ。（例文 4）

During the internship, [can / from / learn / many / things / you / your] mistakes.

_____

(5) 職場では、ポケットに手を入れて話してはいけません。（例文 11）

In the workplace, you [your hands / in / mustn't / pockets / talk / with / your].

_____

(6) 私の両親は東京の郊外でレストランを開店した。（例文 3）

My [have / in / of / opened / parents / a restaurant / a suburb] Tokyo.

_____

(7) 1ヶ月は私たちが新プロジェクトの準備をするには短すぎる。（例文 9）

One month [for / is / prepare / short / to / too / us] for the new project.

_____

(8) その事業をやり遂げるには、2 年間は私たちにとって十分ではない。（例文 7）

Two [accomplish / aren't / enough / for / to / us / years] the project.

_____

英文構造把握問題 　基礎問題 　発展問題 　**文章理解問題**

4. 次の英文を読み、(1) ～ (4) の下線部の語 (句) を並べ替えて、意味の通る英文を作りなさい。

Internships for University Students

University students in Japan usually start to look for a job in their third year of study. Students ask themselves, "What (1)[do / I / in / like / the / to / would] future?" Recently, it is becoming more common for students to take part in internship programs during their time at university. Internships are (2)[choose / for / future / important / students / their / to] careers. During the internship, students can learn many things about working in a company. They learn that they (3)[at / and creatively / earnestly / must / succeed / to / work] a company. Students also learn the skills that are essential in 21st century companies. Nowadays, companies have to utilize new technologies and need young employees with these technological skills. As well as these practical skills, students need to build communication skills. Students often begin working at part-time jobs in their university days. These part-time jobs teach students how to participate actively in society. It is also an opportunity for them to develop their communication skills. This experience is highly appreciated by companies. There (4)[a bright / for / future / highly / in / is / Japan] communicative young people who have knowledge about modern technology.

(1)　[do / I / in / like / the / to / would]

_____

(2)　[choose / for / future / important / students / their / to]

_____

(3)　[at / and creatively / earnestly / must / succeed / to / work]

_____

(4)　[a bright / for / future / highly / in / is / Japan]

_____

unit 11 接続詞（when, because, ifなど）

トピック 衣服、ファッション

||| 解説 |||

　Unit 11では、主文の動詞を修飾する副詞的な文のまとまり（副詞節）を学習します。Unit 10と同様に、基本例文では、副詞的な文のまとまりも便宜的に丸かっこでくくることで、文中での位置をわかりやすくしました。これまで通り、主文の動詞や動詞のまとまりに下線を引きますが、副詞的な文のまとまりの中にも主語と動詞があるので、こちらの動詞や動詞のまとまりにも下線を引きました。副詞的な文のまとまりを作る接続詞などを意識しながら、英作文の練習をしていきましょう。

◀))11

接続詞

時：when（〜とき）

1.　(When I was young) my fashion sense was very unusual.
　　（若かったとき、）私のファッションセンスはとても変わっていた。

時：while（〜間）

2.　Reina didn't care about her appearance (while she was in the U.S.A.)
　　レイナは（アメリカにいる間、）外見を気にしなかった。

時：before（〜前）、after（〜後）

3.　Judy had never worn a kimono (before she came to Japan).
　　ジュディーは（日本に来る前に）一度も着物を着たことがなかった。

時：till（〜まで）、since（〜以来）

4.　Yasuo had never worn a tie (till he started looking for a job).
　　ヤスオは（職探しを始めるまで）一度もネクタイをしたことがなかった。

理由：because（～ので）

5.　I <u>have</u> only essential clothes in my wardrobe (because I'<u>m</u> a minimalist).

　　私は（ミニマリスト<u>なので</u>）洋服だんすには本当に必要な衣類しか<u>持って</u>いない。

条件：if（～たら / なら / れば）

6.　(If I <u>have</u> time tomorrow,) I <u>will buy</u> many clothes at the outlet mall.

　　（もし明日時間が<u>あったら</u>）アウトレットモールでたくさん服を<u>買う</u>つもりだ。

譲歩：though/although（～だが / だけど / けれど）

7.　(Though Kanako <u>isn't</u> very <u>fashion-conscious</u>,) she <u>has</u> many pairs of shoes.

　　（カナコはあまり<u>流行を気にしない</u>けれど、）靴はたくさん<u>持っている</u>。

様態：as/like（～ように）

8.　The idol group members <u>put on</u> their costumes (as they <u>were told</u>).

　　そのアイドルグループのメンバーは（<u>言われたように</u>）衣装を着た。

　　*put on は熟語としてまとめて下線が引かれています。

目的：so that（～ために / ように）

9.　I <u>bought</u> her a wedding dress (so that she <u>can wear</u> it at her wedding ceremony).

　　（結婚式で着ることができるように）彼女にウェディングドレスを<u>買ってあげた</u>。

程度：so～that...（…ほど～だ / とても～なので…）

10.　The kimono <u>was</u> so <u>heavy</u> (that I <u>couldn't wear</u> it).

　　その着物は（着ることができないほど）とても<u>重かった</u>。

　　*その着物はとても<u>重かった</u>ので<u>着ることができなかった</u>。

仮定法

If ＋主語＋be動詞の過去形（were）

11.　(If I <u>were</u> rich,) I <u>would buy</u> a lot of vintage jeans.

　　（もし<u>私が金持ちだったら</u>、）たくさん年代物のジーンズを<u>買う</u>のに。

If ＋主語＋一般動詞の過去形

12.　(If Rina <u>had</u> better fashion sense,) she <u>could be</u> a fashion designer.

　　（もしリナがより良いファッションセンスを<u>持っていたら</u>、）ファッションデザイナーに<u>なれる</u>のに。

1. 次の英文の主語に続く動詞（動詞のまとまり）に下線を引き、副詞的な文のまとまりを意識しながら意味を言いなさい。

(1) If I were you, I would buy more colorful summer clothes. (例文 11)

_____

(2) If I lived in Paris, I would learn about the latest European fashions. (例文 12)

_____

(3) We have to put our winter clothes away because spring has come. (例文 5)

_____

(4) When Masao started job hunting, he was always wearing his new suit. (例文 1)

_____

(5) She had never been interested in fashion until she entered college. (例文 4)

_____

(6) Yuna became famous after she won the beauty contest. (例文 3)

_____

(7) The leather jacket was so expensive that I couldn't afford it. (例文 10)

_____

(8) Long skirts were in fashion while I was at college. (例文 2)

_____

英文構造把握問題　基礎問題　発展問題　文章理解問題

2. 次の [ ] 内の語 (句) を並べ替えて、副詞的な文のまとまりを意識しながら日本文の意味に合う英文を作りなさい。ただし、文頭の語も小文字にしてあります。

(1) もし宝くじに当たったら、彼女に大きなダイヤモンドの指輪を買ってあげるのに。(例文 12)

[buy / her / I / I would / if / the lottery, / won] a large diamond ring.

_____

(2) もし私にもっと勇気があったら、色鮮やかなカーニバル衣装で踊るのに。(例文 11)

[courageous, / dance / I / I would / if / more / were] in a colorful carnival costume.

_____

(3) もし今日クリーニング屋に服を出せば、明日にはそれを受け取れますよ。(例文 6)

[clothes / if / the laundry / send / to / you / your] today, you can get them back tomorrow.

_____

(4) あなたは大学卒業後、仕事でスーツを着なくてはなりません。(例文 3)

After you [college, / from / graduate / have / to / wear / you] a suit for work.

_____

(5) 適した服装を選ぶことができるように服装規定について教えてください。(例文 9)

Tell [about / can / the dress code / I / me / so / that] choose the proper clothes.

_____

(6) マユコはハワイ滞在中、服にたくさんお金を使った。(例文 2)

Mayuko spent [clothes / a lot of / money / on / she / was / while] in Hawaii.

_____

(7) その若いファッションモデルは先輩たちがしたようにステージ上で歩いた。(例文 8)

The young fashion [her / like / model / on / older peers / the stage / walked] did.

_____

(8) 良い高校に入ることができたけれど、制服はそんなにかわいくはなかった。(例文 7)

[although / could / school / a good / high / I / enter], the uniform wasn't so cute.

_____

3. 次の [　] 内の語(句)を並べ替えて、、副詞的な文のまとまりを意識しながら日本文の意味に合う英文を作りなさい。ただし、文頭の語も小文字にしてあります。

(1) 彼女の披露宴に招待されたのだけど、礼服を持っていません。（例文 7）

[her / I / invited / though / to / was / wedding reception], I don't have a formal dress.

_____

(2) 私はそのカリスマCEOが着ているようにいつも地味な黒いTシャツを着ている。（例文 8）

I'm always [CEO / the charismatic / like / a simple / black T-shirt / wearing / wears].

_____

(3) 再流行して以来、私はずっとロングブーツを履き続けている。（例文 4）

I've [back / been / long boots / came / since / they / wearing] into fashion.

_____

(4) 1週間ずっと雨が降り続いているので、服を洗濯できなかった。（例文 5）

I [because / been / my clothes / couldn't / it's / raining / wash] all week.

_____

(5) 寒い冬を乗り切るためにダウンジャケットを探さなくてはならない。（例文 9）

I have to look [can / a down jacket / for / I / so / survive / that] cold winters.

_____

(6) もし彼女と付き合いたいなら、あなたは自分のファッションセンスを磨くべきだ。（例文 6）

If you [go out / her, / should / to / want / with / you] improve your fashion sense.

_____

(7) 私がショートパンツをはいているの見たとき、彼は恥ずかしそうだった。（例文 1）

He [embarrassed / he / looked / me / saw / wearing / when] short pants.

_____

(8) 彼の運動着はとても汚れていたので、何度も洗濯しなければならなかった。（例文 10）

His sportswear was [dirty / had / I / so / that / to / wash] it again and again.

_____

英文構造把握問題　　基礎問題　　発展問題　　**文章理解問題**

4. 次の英文を読み、(1) 〜 (4) の下線部の語 (句) を並べ替えて、意味の通る英文を作りなさい。
ただし、文頭の語も小文字にしてあります。

Clothing and Fashion

Tokyo is one of the fashion capitals of the world. (1)[if / interesting / the most / see / some of / want to / you] and innovative fashion, you should take a look at Tokyo style. There are many kinds of fashion from street wear to high-end designers'. International fashion designers have been watching the street fashion in Tokyo for years and copying the styles. (2)[in / look / Tokyo, / when / you / you can / around you] see people really care about their fashion and clothes. Different areas in Tokyo have different kinds of shops. In Ginza, just near Tokyo station, there are many expensive department stores and the people on the street wear designer brands from the top European fashion houses. People (3)[are / a lot / money / of / spend / they / while] shopping in the department stores of Ginza. In Harajuku, the clothes are cheaper and many cool young people buy their clothes from unique boutiques which line the narrow streets. (4)[I / if / take / a trip / were / I would / you,] to Tokyo to catch up on all the latest styles and experience one of the great fashion capitals of the world.

(1)　[if / interesting / the most / see / some of / want to / you]

_____

(2)　[in / look / Tokyo, / when / you / you can / around you]

_____

(3)　[are / a lot / money / of / spend / they / while]

_____

(4)　[I / if / take / a trip / were / I would / you,]

_____

不定詞（形容詞的用法）、現在分詞、過去分詞

トピック ▶ 飲食

⫿⫿⫿ 解説 ⫿⫿⫿

　Unit 12では形容詞的な語句のまとまり（形容詞句）を含む文に取り組みます。形容詞的な語句のまとまりは名詞を修飾するので、基本例文では、その位置がはっきりするように便宜的に角かっこでくくり、修飾する名詞に波線を引きました。形容詞的な語句のまとまりが主語を修飾する場合、主語と動詞が離れてしまいますが、これまで通り動詞や動詞のまとまりに下線が引かれているので、ここでも主語と動詞の位置をしっかり意識化しましょう。

◀)12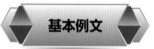

前置詞＋名詞

時

1. The daily set meal [on Wednesday] is fried fish, vegetables, and rice.
   ［水曜日の］日替わりセットは魚のフライと野菜とライスです。

場所

2. All the food [at the Thai restaurant] is very delicious.
   ［そのタイ料理屋の］どの料理もとてもおいしい。

of：A of B ＝ BのA

3. The durian is the king [of tropical fruits].
   ドリアンは［トロピカルフルーツの］王様だ。

その他

4. The cake [with a lot of chestnut topping] is very delicious.
   ［栗がたくさんのっている］そのケーキはとてもおいしい。

不定詞の形容詞的用法

主語関係

5. I need a roommate [to keep me company at mealtimes].

    私は［食事に付き合ってくれる］ルームメートが必要だ。

目的語関係

6. I want a wine [to drink with the main course].

    私は［メイン料理と一緒に飲む］ワインが欲しい。

その他

7. This is a private room [to enjoy your special dinner].

    こちらが［特別ディナーを楽しむための］個室 です。

＋前置詞

8. He needs some money [to buy food with].

    彼は［食べ物を買うための］いくらかのお金を必要としている。

主語を修飾

9. Special desserts [to eat after dinner] will be served soon.

    ［夕食後に食べる］スペシャルデザートがまもなく供されます。

分詞

現在分詞の後置修飾

10. The man [drinking coffee over there] is a famous Italian chef.

    ［あそこでコーヒーを飲んでいる］男性は有名なイタリア人シェフです。

過去分詞の後置修飾

11. Yesterday, I ate a pancake [made by Shiori].

    昨日、私は［シオリが作った］パンケーキを食べた。

    *昨日、私は［シオリによって作られた］パンケーキを食べた。

形容詞

形容詞の後置修飾

12. I know a restaurant [famous for delicious seafood].

    私は［おいしい海鮮料理で有名な］レストランを知っている。

1. 次の英文の主語に続く動詞（動詞のまとまり）に下線を引き、形容詞的な語句のまとまりを意識しながら意味を言いなさい。

(1)　I need somebody to help me cook tonight's dinner.　（例文 5）

_____

(2)　Please give me a recipe for salad dressing to take a look at.　（例文 8）

_____

(3)　My friend always recommends the seafood restaurant near the beach.　（例文 2）

_____

(4)　Her ambition to have her own bakery is quite understandable.　（例文 9）

_____

(5)　The drink popular among young people in Taiwan is bubble tea.　（例文 12）

_____

(6)　The most common fruits in autumn are pears and persimmons.　（例文 1）

_____

(7)　The lunchtime menu of the restaurant changes every day.　（例文 3）

_____

(8)　All the vegetables grown in my garden are so delicious.　（例文 11）

_____

英文構造把握問題　　基礎問題　　発展問題　　文章理解問題

2. 次の [ ] 内の語 (句) を並べ替えて、形容詞的な語句のまとまりを意識しながら日本文の意味に合う英文を作りなさい。ただし、文頭の語も小文字にしてあります。

(1) 彼女にランチをおごってあげる十分なお金がありません。（例文 7）
[buy / don't / have / her / I / enough money / to] lunch.

_____

(2) 私たちは手作りのケーキに乗せるイチゴが必要だ。（例文 6）
[need / on / our / put / strawberries / to / we] home-made cake.

_____

(3) あなたは健康に良いものを食べなくてはなりません。（例文 12）
[eat / for / good / have / something / to / you] your health.

_____

(4) 彼はプリンやヨーグルトのようなやわらかい食べ物が好きだ。（例文 4）
[food / he / like / likes / pudding / soft / or yogurt].

_____

(5) 畑でジャガイモを収穫している男性は私のおじです。（例文 10）
The [the field / harvesting / in / is / man / my / potatoes] uncle.

_____

(6) そのカフェの特別なアイスクリームの味は多くの若者を魅了する。（例文 3）
The [attracts / the cafe's / flavor / ice cream / many / of / special] young people.

_____

(7) トーストに塗られたピーナッツバターは甘すぎた。（例文 11）
The [butter / on / peanut / spread / the / toast / was] too sweet.

_____

(8) 私を海鮮料理フェスに連れて行ってくれるという彼の約束は忘れられてしまった。（例文 9）
[festival / his / me / promise / the seafood / to take / to] was forgotten.

_____

3. 次の [　] 内の語(句)を並べ替えて、形容詞的な語句のまとまりを意識しながら日本文の意味に
合う英文を作りなさい。ただし、文頭の語も小文字にしてあります。

(1) 私は週に1、2回一緒に外食してくれる友達が欲しい。（例文8）

I [eat / a friend / once / out / to / want / with] or twice a week.

_____

(2) 自分のエスニック料理屋店を開くのに協力してくれるスポンサーが見つかった。（例文5）

[found / help / I / me / open / sponsors / to] my own ethnic food restaurant.

_____

(3) 私は台所でオムレツを作っている少年に心惹かれた。（例文10）

I [attracted / the boy / by / cooking / in / an omelet / was] the kitchen.

_____

(4) 今日買っておくべき必要なバーベキュー食材を教えてください。（例文6）

Please let [barbecue / buy / ingredients / know / me / the necessary / to] today.

_____

(5) 我が家で一番人気のある朝食は納豆ご飯です。（例文4）

The [breakfast / family / in / is / most / my / popular] _natto_ and rice.

_____

(6) 冷蔵庫の中の玉子はすでに賞味期限を過ぎてしまった。（例文2）

The [already / eggs / have / in / passed / refrigerator / the] the use-by date.

_____

(7) お正月の伝統的な日本料理は「おせち」と呼ばれる。（例文1）

The traditional [called / during / food / holidays / is / Japanese / the New Year] 'Osechi.'

_____

(8) 私を高級レストランに連れて行く必要はありませんよ。（例文7）

[is / me / need / no / take / there / to] to a fancy restaurant.

_____

英文構造把握問題 　基礎問題 　発展問題 　文章理解問題

4. 次の英文を読み、(1) ～ (4) の下線部の語 (句) を並べ替えて、意味の通る英文を作りなさい。
ただし、文頭の語も小文字にしてあります。

Local Food in Japan

Recently, Japanese food has become popular all over the world. The most
(1)[are / common / countries / foods / in / Japanese / other] sushi and various noodle
dishes. However, many Japanese foods are not available outside of Japan. This is
because they are produced at home, or at small local eateries with locally sourced
ingredients. The seasonal dishes are something you must try when travelling
around Japan. For example, butterbur sprout (*fuki no to*) tempura is common in
spring. The (2)[chance / does / eat / food / a rare / such / to] not come very often. The
local (3)[areas of / different / foods / have / in / Japan / unique] flavors. In Tohoku,
pickled food is more common and the flavors are stronger than in other areas. In
Kyoto, the flavors are more delicate and the beautiful arrangement of seasonal items
draws people's attention. (4)[a fancy / to go / is / need / no / there / to] restaurant
in Japan. It is possible to find delicious, reasonably priced food in many places
in Japan. Make friends with local people and they may take you to some of these
magical local eateries!

(1) [are / common / countries / foods / in / Japanese / other]

_____

(2) [chance / does / eat / food / a rare / such / to]

_____

(3) [areas of / different / foods / have / in / Japan / unique]

_____

(4) [a fancy / to go / is / need / no / there / to]

_____

13 関係代名詞、関係副詞

トピック　住居

‖‖ 解説 ‖‖

　Unit 13 では形容詞的な文のまとまり（形容詞節）を含む文に取り組みます。形容詞的な文のまとまりも名詞を修飾するので、Unit 12 と同様に、基本例文では角かっこでくくり、修飾する名詞に波線を引きました。これまで通り、主文の動詞や動詞のまとまりに下線を引きますが、形容詞的な文のまとまりの中にも主語と動詞があるので、こちらの動詞や動詞のまとまりにも下線を引きました。形容詞的な文を作る文法は関係代名詞と関係副詞なので、それらを含む英作文の練習をしていきましょう。

◀))13　　基本例文

関係代名詞

who（主格）　修飾する名詞が人

1.　Misaki is the girl [who is proud of her hometown's World Heritage Site].
　　ミサキは［自分の故郷の世界遺産を誇りに思っている］少女 だ。

whom（目的格）　修飾する名詞が人

2.　She is the student [whom most residents of the dormitory admire].
　　彼女は［ほとんどの寮生が賞賛する］学生 だ。
　　*whom の代わりに who が使われることもよくあります。

whose（所有格）　修飾する名詞が人

3.　I have a friend [whose house is gorgeous].
　　私には［家が豪華な］友だちがいる。

which（主格）　修飾する名詞が人以外のものやこと

4.　This is the town [which has a lot of sightseeing spots].
　　こちらが［たくさん観光名所のある］町 です。

---

which（目的格）	修飾する名詞が人以外のものやこと

5. The condominium [which we saw last week] was already sold.

[私たちが先週見学した] マンションはすでに売約済みだった。

---

whose（所有格）	修飾する名詞が人以外のものやこと

6. I saw a house [whose roof was totally covered with solar panels].

私は [屋根が全てソーラーパネルで覆われている] 家を見た。

関係代名詞の省略（目的格）

7. The city [I like the most in the world] is Vancouver.

[世界で一番好きな] 都市はバンクーバーです。

＊目的格の関係代名詞は、修飾する名詞が人でもものやことでも省略できます。

前置詞＋関係代名詞

8. These are the logs [with which he is going to build his lodge].

これらは、[彼がロッジを建てるのに使う予定の] 丸太 です。

関係副詞

when

9. I clearly remember the day [when we bought our condominium].

[私たちがマンションを購入した] 日のことをはっきりと覚えている。

---

where

10. This is the town [where I was born and raised].

ここが [私が生まれ育った] 町 です。

---

why

11. I didn't know the reason [why she moved to this town].

私は [彼女がこの町に引っ越してきた] 理由がわからなかった。

---

howの省略

12. That is the way [he found his apartment near the university].

それが [彼が大学近くにアパートを見つけた] 方法 です。

1. 次の英文の主語に続く動詞（動詞のまとまり）に下線を引き、形容詞的な文のまとまりを意識しながら意味を言いなさい。

(1)　I have a friend whose hometown is far away from here. （例文 3）

_____

(2)　I moved to the coast where I can enjoy surfing every day. （例文 10）

_____

(3)　The girl whom I met on the train lives with me in the shared house now. （例文 2）

_____

(4)　People who love their hometown usually have many good friends there. （例文 1）

_____

(5)　This is the most reasonable apartment I have ever found. （例文 7）

_____

(6)　This is the way I solved the trouble with my neighbors. （例文 12）

_____

(7)　The cottage which I visited last winter was warm and cozy. （例文 5）

_____

(8)　What is the reason why you want to sell your condominium? （例文 11）

_____

英文構造把握問題　基礎問題　発展問題　文章理解問題

2. 次の [　] 内の語 (句) を並べ替えて、形容詞的な文のまとまりを意識しながら日本文の意味に合う英文を作りなさい。ただし、文頭の語も小文字にしてあります。

(1) 私は父が今ニューヨークに住んでいる少女を知っている。（例文 3）

I [father / a girl / in / know / lives / New York / whose] now.

(2) 私には彼が高層住宅に住みたい理由がわかりません。（例文 11）

I [don't / he / know / the reason / to / wants / why] live in a high-rise apartment.

(3) 私の親友は台所がとても小さいアパートに住んでいる。（例文 6）

My best friend [an apartment / in / is / kitchen / lives / very small / whose].

(4) 壊れた塀を修理している人は私のおじです。（例文 1）

[the broken / fence / is / person / repairing / the / who] is my uncle.

(5) こちらが彼が大量の漫画のコレクションを保管している部屋です。（例文 8）

[he / in / is / keeps / the room / this / which] his large collection of comic books.

(6) 2 年前に借りたアパートはとても古かった。（例文 5）

The [ago / apartment / I / rented / was / which / two years] very old.

(7) 月曜と木曜がゴミ出しをする日ですよ。（例文 9）

Monday and Thursday [are / the days / the garbage / should / take / when / you] out.

(8) 横浜は若いカップルの間で人気のある町です。（例文 4）

[among / is / is popular / the / town / which / Yokohama] young couples.

3. 次の [ ] 内の語(句)を並べ替えて、形容詞的な文のまとまりを意識しながら日本文の意味に合う英文を作りなさい。

(1) 私はバルコニーが美しい海に面している新しいアパートが大好きだ。(例文 6)

I [new apartment / balcony / facing / is / love / my / whose] the beautiful ocean.

_____

(2) 私は彼女の話し方から出身地を当てることができます。(例文 12)

I can [from / her / hometown / identify / she / speaks / the way].

_____

(3) 私は美しい山々に囲まれた町に住みたい。(例文 4)

I want to live [beautiful / by / in / is / surrounded / a town / which] mountains.

_____

(4) あなたが新居に引っ越す日にちを教えてください。(例文 9)

Please [the date / me / move / tell / when / will / you] to your new house.

_____

(5) 彼女が家の設計をお願いした人は有名な建築家だ。(例文 2)

The person [asked / design / her house / is / she / to / whom] a famous architect.

_____

(6) こちらが私の家に入ることができる鍵です。(例文 8)

This [can / enter / is / the key / which / with / you] my house.

_____

(7) あの家を買うのに私たちが工面できるお金はこれが全てです。(例文 7)

This [afford / all / can / is / the money / to / we] buy that house.

_____

(8) 東京の繁華街は私が最も心地よく感じることのできる場所です。(例文 10)

Downtown Tokyo [can / feel / I / is / place / the / where] most comfortable.

_____

英文構造把握問題 | 基礎問題 | 発展問題 | 文章理解問題

4. 次の英文を読み、(1) ～ (4) の下線部の語 (句) を並べ替えて、意味の通る英文を作りなさい。
ただし、文頭の語も小文字にしてあります。

The Historic City of York

York is a beautiful city in the north of England. It is also my hometown. York has many famous places to visit and sights to see. The most famous is York Minster which is a beautifully decorated church with amazing sculptures. The stunning white stone minster can be seen from miles away. You will never forget the sight of it when you have seen it. The city is surrounded by (1)[enemies / keep / to / used / wall / which / a wide] out. However, now the wall is full of people walking around the city sightseeing. It is common for tourists to take a boat ride along the River Ouse. (2)[are / elegant / glide / many / swans / there / which] gracefully along the river. Traditional shops can be found all over York which sell local products. There are also many museums which tell the famous history of this fantastic city. At York Railway Museum, you can see old fashioned steam trains and even a Japanese bullet train. The (3)[are / friendly / meet in / people / whom / York / you] and welcoming. York is (4)[can / city / feel / history / an incredible / where / you] all around you.

(1)　[enemies / keep / to / used / wall / which / a wide]

_____

(2)　[are / elegant / glide / many / swans / there / which]

_____

(3)　[are / friendly / meet in / people / whom / York / you]

_____

(4)　[can / city / feel / history / an incredible / where / you]

_____

復習問題
(Unit 8 ～ 13)

1. Unit 8 の例文を参考に、次の [　] 内の語 (句) を並べ替えて、名詞的な語句のまとまりを意識しながら日本文の意味に合う英文を作りなさい。ただし、文頭の語も小文字にしてあります。尚、以下の問題で扱っているトピックは「衣服、ファッション」になります。

(1) 私は有名ブティックがたくさん並ぶあの通りを歩くことが好きだ。(例文 8)

[along / full / I / like / street / that / walking] of famous boutiques.

_____

(2) 私はあの高価な革のジャケットを買おうか買うまいか迷う。(例文 12)

[buy / expensive / I / that / to / whether / wonder] leather jacket or not.

_____

(3) 私は次の就職面接にどのネクタイをしていくか決めなくてはならない。(例文 11)

[decide / have to / I / tie / to / wear / which] to the next job interview.

_____

(4) 彼女はパーティー用のドレスに何色を選んだらいいか考え続けている。(例文 10)

[choose / color / kept / she / thinking / to / what] for her party dress.

_____

(5) そのパーティーにふさわしい服装規定を知ることは私にとって重要だ。(例文 4)

It [for / important / is / know / me / the proper / to] dress code for the party.

_____

(6) こんな素敵なセーターをくれるとはあなたは親切ですね。(例文 5)

It [give / is / kind / me / of / to / you] such a wonderful sweater.

_____

(7) 私の将来の夢は世界で有名なファッションデザイナーになることだ。(例文 1)

[be / dream / a famous / future / is / my / to] fashion designer around the world.

_____

(8) 職場でのふだん着の着用が私たちをより快適な気分にしてくれた。(例文 6)

[casual / clothes / in / made / the office / us / wearing] feel more comfortable.

_____

2. Unit 9 の例文を参考に、次の [　] 内の語 (句) を並べ替えて、名詞的な文のまとまりを意識しながら日本文の意味に合う英文を作りなさい。ただし、文頭の語も小文字にしてあります。尚、以下の問題で扱っているトピックは「飲食」になります。

(1) 彼女がインド料理屋のどの料理も気に入ってくれたことが嬉しい。（例文 4）
[all / the food / glad / I'm / liked / she / that] at the Indian restaurant.

―――――――――――――――――――――――――――――――

(2) 北海道でたくさん新鮮なカニを食べることができたらなあ。（例文 7）
I [could / eat / fresh / I / a lot / of / wish] crab in Hokkaido.

―――――――――――――――――――――――――――――――

(3) チエコは海鮮料理が好きなのだろうか。（例文 12）
[Chieko / I / likes / or / seafood / whether / wonder] not.

―――――――――――――――――――――――――――――――

(4) 昨夜、彼がどのくらいたくさんお酒を飲んだか私にはわからない。（例文 11）
[alcohol / don't / he / how / I / know / much] drank last night.

―――――――――――――――――――――――――――――――

(5) どこでその有名な露天市を見つけることができるか教えてください。（例文 9）
Please [can / find / I / know / let / me / where] the famous open-air market.

―――――――――――――――――――――――――――――――

(6) 健康のためにもっと野菜を食べるべきだとアサミは私に言った。（例文 3）
Asami [eat / I / me / more / should / that / told] vegetables for my health.

―――――――――――――――――――――――――――――――

(7) 友人がそのテーマパークでどのレストランが一番安いか教えてくれた。（例文 10）
My [friend / is / me / restaurant / the / told / which] cheapest at the theme park.

―――――――――――――――――――――――――――――――

(8) 彼女が 50 以上のハーブやスパイスを集めてきたことは驚きだ。（例文 5）
[collected / has / it's / more / she / surprising / that] than 50 herbs and spices.

―――――――――――――――――――――――――――――――

3. Unit 10 の例文を参考に、次の [ ]内の語 (句) を並べ替えて、副詞的な語句のまとまりを意識しながら日本文の意味に合う英文を作りなさい。ただし、文頭の語も小文字にしてあります。尚、以下の問題で扱っているトピックは「住居」になります。

(1) 近所の人たちに迷惑をかけないよう私は夜、ピアノは弾かない。（例文 10）
[annoy / don't / I / the neighbors, / not / play / to] the piano at night.

_____

(2) 私はアパートを探しながら、その町をずっと歩き続けている。（例文 12）
[around / been / for / I've / looking / the town, / walking] an apartment.

_____

(3) 在宅勤務ができるとは彼はなんとラッキーなのか！（例文 7）
How lucky [able to / be / from / he / is / to / work] home!

_____

(4) 彼女は父親がロッジを建てているのを見てわくわくした。（例文 6）
[building / excited / her father / see / she / to / was] a lodge.

_____

(5) 彼はのんびり暮らすために田舎に家を買った。（例文 5）
[bought / the countryside / he / a house / in / live / to] comfortably.

_____

(6) 彼は春休み中に良いアパートを見つけたいと思っている。（例文 2）
He wants [apartment / break / during / find / a nice / the spring / to].

_____

(7) ミナコは4月からシェアハウスに入居するほど十分勇気がある。（例文 8）
Minako [courageous / enough / house / is / move into / a shared / to] from April.

_____

(8) そのマンションは私たちが購入するには高すぎた。（例文 9）
The [condominium / expensive / for / to / too / us / was] buy.

_____

英文構造把握問題　基礎問題　発展問題　文章理解問題　**復習問題**

4.　Unit 11 の例文を参考に、次の [　] 内の語 (句) を並べ替えて、副詞的な文のまとまりを意識しながら日本文の意味に合う英文を作りなさい。ただし、文頭の語も小文字にしてあります。尚、以下の問題で扱っているトピックは「健康」になります。

(1)　私は健康が維持できるように毎朝散歩をしている。（例文 9）

I take [can / I / keep / every morning / so / that / a walk] healthy.

_____

(2)　私はひどく疲れていたが、朝早く起きた。（例文 7）

[although / got / I / I was / tired, / up / very] early in the morning.

_____

(3)　温泉でリラックスしたかったので、私は箱根を訪れた。（例文 5）

I [because / Hakone / I / relax / to / visited / wanted] in the hot springs.

_____

(4)　もし十分な時間があったら、ヨガ教室に通うのに。（例文 12）

I [attend / had / I / if / school / would / a yoga] enough time.

_____

(5)　もしお金持ちだったら、南国の海辺のリゾート地で気分転換するのに。（例文 11）

[I / I would / if / myself / refresh / rich, / were] at a tropical seaside resort.

_____

(6)　言われたとおりに毎食後、この薬を飲んでください。（例文 8）

Please [after / as / each meal / this medicine / take / were / you] told.

_____

(7)　ヒトシは若かった頃、健康ではなかった。（例文 1）

Hitoshi wasn't [good / he / health / in / was / when / young].

_____

(8)　頭痛があまりにもひどくて私は何もすることができなかった。（例文 10）

My headache [couldn't / do / I / severe / so / that / was] anything.

_____

5. Unit 12の例文を参考に、次の[ ]内の語 (句) を並べ替えて、形容詞的な語句のまとまりを意識しながら日本文の意味に合う英文を作りなさい。ただし、文頭の語も小文字にしてあります。尚、以下の問題で扱っているトピックは「異性、恋愛」になります。

(1) 私は次のデートを成功させるための何かアドバイスが欲しい。（例文 7）

[some advice / next date / I / make / my / need / to] successful.

_____

(2) 私はクリスマスイブに一緒にいる彼氏を見つけたいと思っている。（例文 8）

[be / a boyfriend / to find / hoping / I'm / to / with] on Christmas Eve.

_____

(3) 私は恋人と飲む良いワインを見つけなくてはならない。（例文 6）

[drink / find / a good / have to / I / to / wine] with my sweetheart.

_____

(4) 幸運なことに、野球の試合に連れて行ってくれるいい人が見つかった。（例文 5）

Luckily, [found / guy / I / me / a nice / take / to] to a baseball game.

_____

(5) あそこで本を読んでいる男の子は私の彼氏です。（例文 10）

[a book / boy / is / over / reading / the / there] my boyfriend.

_____

(6) クラスで女子に一番人気のある男の子はタカシです。（例文 4）

The [among / boy / the girls / in / most / my / popular] class is Takashi.

_____

(7) ガールフレンドが作ってくれたカレーライスはとてもおいしかった。（例文 11）

The curry and [by / delicious / my girlfriend / made / rice / so / was].

_____

(8) プロポーズをするという彼の計画は見事に実行された。（例文 9）

His [make / a marriage / plan / proposal / successfully / to / was] carried out.

_____

英文構造把握問題　基礎問題　発展問題　文章理解問題　**復習問題**

6. Unit 13の例文を参考に、次の[　]内の語 (句) を並べ替えて、形容詞的な文のまとまりを意識しながら日本文の意味に合う英文を作りなさい。ただし、文頭の語も小文字にしてあります。尚、以下の問題で扱っているトピックは「仕事」になります。

(1) 私は就職の面接を受けた日のことをはっきりと覚えている。（例文 9）

I clearly [day / I / interviewed / remember / the / was / when] for the job.

_____

(2) あなたがその会社で働くことを選んだ理由を教えてくだい。（例文 11）

[chose / me / the reason / tell / to / why / you] work for the company.

_____

(3) 彼は評判が着実に高まっている会社に職を得た。（例文 6）

He [a company / got / in / a job / reputation / was / whose] steadily growing.

_____

(4) 彼女はきわめて内容の濃い職業訓練コースをちょうど終えたところだ。（例文 4）

She [finished / has / a job / just / training course / was / which] extremely intense

_____

(5) 佐々木氏はその会社で新しいプロジェクトを始めた人だ。（例文 1）

Mr. Sasaki [is / man / the new / project / started / the / who] in the company.

_____

(6) それが新しい顧客を見つけることができる最善の方法です。（例文 12）

[best / can / find / that's / the / way / you] new customers.

_____

(7) 彼女が選んだインターンシップは自分にとって良い経験になるでしょう。（例文 7）

[be / chosen / has / internship / she / the / will] a good experience for her.

_____

(8) 四谷は私が4月から働く場所だ。（例文 10）

Yotsuya [going / I'm / is / the place / to / where / work] from April.

_____

体系的アプローチで身につける
基礎英作文

検印
省略 ©2023 年 1 月 31 日　第 1 版発行

編著者　　　　　　　　羽井佐　昭彦
　　　　　　　　　　　Gary Bourke
　　　　　　　　　　　Joanne Sato

発行者　　　　　　　　小川　洋一郎
発行所　　　　　　株式会社 朝日出版社
〒101-0065 東京都千代田区西神田 3-3-5
電話　東京　(03) 3239-0271
FAX　東京　(03) 3239-0479
E-mail　text-e@asahipress.com
振替口座　00140-2-46008
http://www.asahipress.com/
組版／メディアアート　製版／錦明印刷

ISBN 978-4-255-15707-8